Spontaneous Revivals

Asbury College 1905-2006

Firsthand Accounts of Lives Transformed

Robert J. Kanary

"No more let sins and sorrows grow, nor thorns infest the ground;
He comes to make His blessings flow, far as the curse is found."

Joy to the World, by Isaac Watts (1674-1748)

Printed by CreateSpace, and Amazon.com company
ISBN-9781542673785

Visit Website:
www.robertkanarybooks.com

Cover design and layout 2016 by Kyle J. Schroeder

PREFACE

Why Produce an Anthology of this Sort?

"Probably no major campus in America has experienced revival more frequently than Asbury College"[1] said Dr. Wesley Duewel, a former president of One Mission Society. Approximately a dozen spontaneous demonstrations of God's presence, power, and love occurred over the years. Asbury revivals follow a similar pattern (summary below).

Catalogue of ASBURY COLLEGE, 1906-1907

A VERITABLE PENTECOST AT WILMORE, KENTUCKY*

The following facts distinguish it from any and all other meetings I have attended in a period of thirty-five years:
1) It was unplanned and unexpected.
2) The absolute absence of human leadership.
3) It occupies everybody and all our wakeful hours.
4) Students are called for foreign mission work.
5) Unusual profound conviction pervades the assembly. The entire chapel is an altar.
6) Not one indecorous thing has yet been done or indiscreet word uttered amid all this holy recklessness and divine order.

I haven't told half the story. It cannot be told in human words. I wish I could portray its grandeur, its glory and its graciousness. The work is not a week old yet. I know not when it will close.

Dr. B. F. Haynes, Pages 10-12, Abridged

This book is a collection of eyewitness accounts from people who experienced and were shaped by these divine visitations. Their stories come from published, unpublished, and personal interviews.

People tell stories of the past for many reasons. First, they may cherish a legacy. *"And now that I am old and gray-headed, O God, do not forsake me, till I make your strength known to this generation and Your power to all who are to come"* (Psalm 71:18).

Where there is divine activity, we have an obligation to share, *"that the generations to come might know, and the children yet unborn; that they in turn might tell it to their children; so that they might put their trust in God, and not forget the deeds of God, but keep His commandments..."* (Psalm 78:5-7). God wants remembrance.

Second, sacred memories can become vague or unknown over time. In 2015 I spent two months in Wilmore, Kentucky, home of Asbury University, as part of a one-year sabbatical. I conducted informal interviews with current students and recent graduates, asking what they know about Asbury's revival heritage. In most cases, they knew little. But tell them a story or two—including the fact that chapel time was extended and classes suspended, sometimes for a whole week—and they are fascinated. I find people are eager to listen.

Third, and most importantly, God uses the witness of the past to inspire renewed passion for prayer and divine visitation. Revival begins and ends with prayer. Dr. J. Edwin Orr wrote, *"There have been instances in the history of the church when the telling and retelling of the wonderful works of God have been used to rekindle the expectations of the faithful intercessors and prepare the way for another Awakening."*[2] Remembrance and retelling act as a spark.

An attempt has been made for this anthology to be representative in nature, honest, objective and balanced. Some years may be characterized as "Mega Revivals" (1950 and 1970, about which two books have been written). But every revival and every individual account is unique. No story is too insignificant or too small. Each one represents a profound reorientation of values and beliefs. God revitalized individuals and the college, causing revitalization to overflow into the world beyond.

Some Special Features

Periodically, the anthology features brief pieces related to historical, theological, and programmatic points of interest. For instance, parallels may be drawn between one episode from *The Chronicles of Narnia,* by C.S. Lewis, and the existence of the divine.

Another example is the inclusion of a description of the *John Wesley Great Experiment* which played a significant role as a prelude to the 1970 revival.

Additional variety appears in the form of occasional sidebars, small thematic collections entitled "snapshots," and a visual chart—the first of four addenda. We trust God guided in the choosing and editing of selections.

Many individuals assisted with this project. Special thanks to Asbury Archives Director Suzanne Gehring, retired professors Mark Elliot (history) and Beth Gardner (English), graphic design assistant Kyle Schroeder, and Seedbed Press editor Andrew Miller. Others receive mention in the acknowledgements at the conclusion of this volume.

At times I felt like a Levite in God's temple, handling sacred objects, in this case sacred memories. I hope they inspire readers to reconnect with their own personal experiences.

"Revivals are sovereign works of God, but are always related to the obedience of God's people. Are you and I willing to prepare the way of the Lord by prayer, fasting, and obedience?"[3]

[1]Wesley Duewel, *Revival Fire* (Grand Rapids, MI: Zondervan, 1995), p. 331.

[2]J. Edwin Orr, *Tongues Aflame: The Impact of 20th Century Revivals* (Chicago: Moody Press, 1973), p. viii.

[3]Wesley Duewel, *Revival Fire*, p. 17.

TABLE OF CONTENTS

Preface

Table of Contents

John Wesley Hughes - 1890

INTRODUCTION: Where did it all begin? In a sense the Asbury revivals started with the personal Pentecost of Rev. John Wesley Hughes and his wife, Mary W. Hughes. It is replete with agonizing prayer and total surrender. They are like Abraham and Sarah, imperfect but chosen human vessels, the root of all that follows. Their journey began with fear and trembling, but it blossomed into bold and unapologetic obedience to the Spirit of God. This piece is abridged from chapter ten of his autobiography.[1]

After twelve years in the pastorate and one in the evangelistic field I received a clarion call to college work. Of all calls this was the most unthought-of, unexpected, and undesired.... My call to college work was clear, but bewildering as I considered what seemed my utter inability and unfitness.

I had seen and felt the need for years of *a real salvation school* where religious young men and women could hold their salvation; and where unsaved and unsanctified students would not only be encouraged, but urged to get saved and sanctified and prepared educationally for their life's work....

This would be a school where the religious atmosphere might be such that the students would recognize the world's need and willingly obey the Lord's command. "But when He saw the multitude He was moved with compassion on them, because they fainted and were scattered abroad as sheep having no shepherd. Then said He unto His disciples, 'The harvest is plenteous, but the laborers are few, pray ye therefore the Lord of the harvest that He will send forth laborers into His harvest'" (Matthew 9:36-38).

I believed then, as I do now, that a rounded and complete education involved a genuine Christian experience. To educate the body to the neglect of the mind and the soul makes a man beastly. To educate the mind to the neglect of body and soul leads to dead intellectualism. To educate the soul to the neglect of mind and body results in fanaticism.

I also believed then, as I do now, that a real Christian school would put the Bible in the curriculum, teaching the history, doctrine, and experience of our holy Christianity daily, stressing the teaching of Jesus, "Seek ye first the kingdom of God and His righteousness, and all these things shall be added unto you" (Matthew 6:33). For many years I had been sending young men and women, full of faith and the Holy Ghost, out of my revivals to colleges to get them prepared for the Master's service. A great percent of them, as they do now, got their faith destroyed and lost their religious experience and the call of God to the ministry and other Christian work.

One day as I sat in the old Kentucky Central Depot, Lexington, Kentucky, having been from my home in Carlisle, Kentucky, for a month in evangelistic work, God not only gave me a vision of a real salvation school, but called me to the work. I purchased my ticket for Carlisle, my home. I got on the train and pulled my hat down over my face so that no one could interfere with my prayer and meditation till I reached my destination.

I spent part of the time in the bosom of my family with my wife and three children, but I spent hours each day in my room in agonizing prayer with heavy heart and perplexed mind, hoping in some way to rid myself of what seemed to me a fearful responsibility, one that I was in no way prepared to shoulder. I hoped and prayed that God would relieve me of the burden, but as I could get no relief from that direction, I was hopeful that my wife, who had been so faithful and true to me in my work, both in the pastorate and evangelical fields, would enter her protest against my entrance into this untried field. So I called her to my room.

When she came in I was on my face upon the floor praying God to help me break the news to her so as to bring right results. She sat down on the floor by me. I said to her, "I have a matter on my mind to which I must call your *undivided* attention." With her characteristic quietness and frankness, she said, "I am all ears and eyes and will hear what you have to say." When she gave that answer, which implied her willingness to follow me where God would lead, I burst into tears and told her about my call to college work and how perplexed I was over it. Her unexpected answer was, "When I married you, I did it with the understanding that I would follow you into every line of work to which God called you." I felt then that my last prop had fallen and that I could do nothing but obey God and hope and pray for success in our new divinely appointed field. We at once began to pray and to plan for the beginning of our new project.

The news soon got out that I was about to start a college to be known as a holiness school; that in connection with the college curriculum the Bible would be placed as a regular textbook; and that its history, doctrines, and experiences, as revealed in Bible characters, would be taught and emphasized as other textbooks. Also the work of the day would be opened with an earnest religious chapel service—in reading and expounding the Scriptures, singing, praying, and testifying as the Lord would lead. Each teacher would be required to open class with an invocation by teacher or pupil....

When I began to advertise the school, a college president said to me: "What is your *objective*?" I answered, "A *sure enough religious school.*" "Have you an announcement of the school?" I handed him my first four-page circular. It began as follows:

> INTRODUCTORY: Feeling the great need of a distinctively religious school where young men and young women can get a thorough college education under the direction of a faculty composed of men and women wholly consecrated to God, we have decided to open "Kentucky Holiness School" at Wilmore, eighteen miles south of Lexington, on the Cincinnati Southern Railroad, near High Bridge. The school will open September 2 with three teachers. Other teachers will be employed when the patronage demands it.... We expect the hearty co-operation of holiness people everywhere. We feel satisfied that the work is of God, and will succeed.

When he read the introduction to my circular, it offended him. He then said, "What do you *mean* by '*distinctively religious school*'?" I answered, "I mean a school in which the doctrines and experiences are taught and emphasized daily so as to lead the young men and women to forsake sin and give themselves wholly to God." His reply to that was, "If you mean that fanaticism called 'sanctification,' we endeavor to destroy it." My reply to him was, "I think you succeed as well as any crowd I ever knew." I said, "Furthermore, we will endeavor as a faculty to do all in our power to lead our students to the Bible experiences of regeneration and entire sanctification and to live daily a consecrated, holy life with warm hearts and cool heads, always endeavoring to tear down the works of the devil and to build up the Kingdom of God." I have had no occasion since that day to retract my *Objective*.

[1]John Wesley Hughes, *The Autobiography of John Wesley Hughes, D.D., Founder of Asbury and Kingswood Colleges, with Biographical Contributions by Rev. Andrew Johnson, D.D., Ph.D. and Appreciations by Others* (Louisville, KY: Pentecostal Publishing Company, 1923), pp. 99-105. Used by Permission Asbury Theological Seminary, Reprint by First Fruits Press (Wilmore, KY: 2013).

SNAPSHOTS – Early Years

Location, Location, Location.   In 1790, Francis Asbury launched Bethel Academy three miles southeast of present-day Wilmore. Returning on October 4, 1800, he lamented the choice of location. "Saturday, I came to Bethel, Cokesbury College in miniature *[NOTE: Founded in Maryland in 1787, Cokesbury closed in 1796]*, eighty by thirty feet, three stories, with a high roof, and finished below. Now we want a fund and an income of three hundred per year to carry it on; without which it will be useless. But it is too distant from public places; its being surrounded by the river Kentucky in part, we now find to be no benefit: thus all our excellencies are turned into defects." *Francis Asbury, Journals.*

The Name. At its inception in 1890 the original name was Kentucky Holiness College, but Rev. Hughes was forced to look for another because his bishop protested that every Methodist college is a holiness school. Hughes's chagrin turned to delight when he discovered that in 1790 Bishop Francis Asbury founded the first Methodist college west of the Appalachian Mountains, the defunct Bethel Academy, just a few miles away. He felt this was providential, and so adopted the name Asbury College. *The Autobiography of John Wesley Hughes.*

E. A. Ferguson and an Anonymous College Reporter - 1905

INTRODUCTION: The following remarks appeared in late February, 1905, on the pages of the Pentecostal Herald.[1] *They are the earliest printed record of a revival bearing marks of the spontaneous pattern rather than the "constituted means" pattern [see page 8]. If the information had been untrue, people in Wilmore would have been in a position to refute it. Rev. Ferguson was apparently a traveling preacher and the article—even if not an exaggeration—could be construed as an advertisement. In any case, something unusual happened even by the standards of a holiness college.*

WILMORE, KY. - All glory and praise to our God forever! We are in a mighty sweep of victory here. God has again given us one of the best meetings of our lives. This meeting is a joint meeting of school and church, held in the M.E. Church, South, Brother Humphrey, pastor. The school is practically closed. Classrooms are turned into altar services, and the students are not only being saved there, but in their rooms. The house and altars are filled at every service and a great number have either been saved, reclaimed, or sanctified. Rev. J. W. Hughes, the president, says that it is one of the best, if not the greatest, meetings in the history of Asbury College; the faculty and the people say the same. God, through His word and Spirit, has dug up sin and given us a mighty upheaval and confession of sin where it had been covered up. Lodges, tobacco, adultery, all get a black eye. The faculty works day and night to get pupils saved, and they are seeing their prayers answered. Prof. C.A. Bromley, Revs. J. B. Kendall, C. M. Humphrey, Maxwell, Pickett, Harris, Jones, and others have been used of God to push the battle.

As ever in Holy Love, E. A. Ferguson

NOTE: The second account appeared in the Herald during the autumn semester, November, 1905.[2] Mention is made of a "glorious revival" that started in the Boys' Conference (later renamed the Ministerial Association).

ASBURY COLLEGE NOTES - We are now well into the second month *[NOTE: October 1905]* of the sixteenth annual session of Asbury College, and the school never had a more prosperous year in its history than the present one is proving. There was never a sweeter, deeper, pro-founder, and more all-pervasive spiritual atmosphere than now prevails in the institution. There is a great spirit of prayer throughout the student body, and victories are coming daily through this channel. A gracious revival which began in the Boys' Conference and continued two weeks closed a few nights ago. Besides the results beyond the pale of the school, fifteen young gentleman and young ladies among the students were either converted or sanctified, and one of the young men has since the meeting felt called to the mission field.

The missionary spirit of the school is truly apostolic in intensity and fervor. The study of missions is systematically and diligently pursued. The daily noon prayer meeting centers on the theme of foreign missions; and the music of the heartfelt prayers, songs and shouts that are borne forth daily from the walls are soul-stirring.

CONCLUSION: For somewhat obscure reasons, the college Board of Trustees nominated a new president about the time of the spring revival. John Wesley Hughes was forced to vacate his position as founding president. The board begged his continuance as a professor but he declined.

As the fall semester began, the new administration would surely want to reassure their wider constituency that life was "better than ever" at the college, spring reports of "heaven come down" notwithstanding. For the most part the students were happy. Regardless of administrative upheavals, school leaders continued their dual commitments to "Eruditio et Religio," i.e. scholarship and spiritual life inseparably intertwined. The stage was being set for the "mega" revival of 1907.

[1]*The Pentecostal Herald*, Wednesday, Feb. 22, 1905, p. 9.

[2]*The Pentecostal Herald,* Wednesday, Nov. 1 [5], 1905, p. 13.

Buildings.   Construction on the first building—located on six acres on Main Street—began in July, 1890. It was simple, essentially a two-story box divided into four rooms. It required only a few weeks to build. When the cornerstone of the first administration building was laid in 1900, it contained a piece of stone from the ruins of the original Bethel Academy. By comparison, in 2017 the college—now a university—has expanded to 43 buildings, along with other holdings such as an equine center. ATL*

Rural Situation.   By 1890 rail access created new opportunities. The beautiful bluegrass—with its remote rural environment— was considered advantageous to physical and moral health. Access to the wider world was changing. On August 19, 1903, the first automobile arrived in Wilmore. Passenger trains were still operating in the mid 1960s, but are now a relic of the past. ATL

Balancing Christianity and Culture

HOLINESS MEETING. "Every Monday evening there is held in the college chapel a service especially given to instruction in the doctrines of regeneration and entire sanctification. Part of the service is usually given to testimony. As the close of each service there is an opportunity given to anyone who wishes to seek pardon or purity. All students are required to attend these services." [*NOTE: Spontaneous revivals usually begin at colleges with required student chapel services.]* ATL

LITERARY SOCIETIES. "In the Autumn of 1902, the Columbian and Athenian Literary Societies were organized. The purpose of these societies is to develop in their members literary taste, talent, and the giving of that culture and breadth of vision which can be obtained only by acquaintance with the best literature and the interchange of thought between wide-awake and aggressive minds." ATL

*ATL—Indicates information source is the online Asbury University Timeline, developed by Dr. William E. McKinley. Go to: https://www.asbury.edu/about-us/history. Incidentally, a somewhat more sophisticated visually interactive timeline is available. Go to: https://www.asbury.edu/timeline#vars!date=1985-01-01_05:37:48!. Both accessed 3/31/16.

Note: AUA—Indicates source is available in the Asbury University Archives.

PLANNED AND SPONTANEOUS REVIVALS

Adapted from an essay by Dr. Harold E. Raser, Asbury College, 1979.[1]

There are two different revival traditions. Although they have elements in common that overlap and complement each other they are still distinguishable.

The first is <u>SPONTANEOUS</u>. It is extraordinary in a number of ways: surprising suddenness, number of people affected, and the depth of impact.

In 1737 Jonathan Edwards published an account of one such awakening. It started in his New England congregation and flowed out into many other communities and became known as the "First Great Awakening." In 1739 John Wesley read this account and was astounded. Soon after a similar move of God came to England, and Methodism in its various forms became the foremost representative.

The Second is <u>PLANNED</u>. It is planned insofar as people use a variety of means or techniques to prepare and stage the revival, which if done in good faith yields fruit for God.

The chief exponent of planned revival was Charles Finney. Toward the close of the "Second Great Awakening" (which began about 1801 and faded out before mid-century), Finney developed ways to conduct revivals by "constituted means" ordained by God. In other words, people can help bring about revivals: these are less spontaneous but are used by God.

Asbury has seen its share of planned revivals. What is surprising is the number of the rarer spontaneous type, the theme of this collection.

[1]*Dr. Harold E. Raser, a professor in the Division of Philosophy and Religion at Asbury College, wrote his essay in 1979. A more extended section of his work is found in Addendum #2 at the conclusion of this anthology.*

Benjamin Haynes – 1907

INTRODUCTION: Dr. Benjamin Haynes was President of Asbury College from 1905 to 1908. He contributed the following two sets of remarks to a newspaper. An editor at Asbury reprinted the account in The Catalogue of Asbury College 1906-1907 *(a look back at the previous year) and* Eighteenth Announcement 1907-1908 *(looking forward).[1] Readers will note a general pattern and characteristics that appear in subsequent revivals. President Haynes underscores how a spirit of praise characterized this revival.*

A PHENOMENAL YEAR

...Dr. B. Carradine conducted a great revival in the college chapel in the Fall [1906] which God most wonderfully blessed. Salvation work has continually gone on. Early in the spring term [1907] the Spirit gradually deepened in His hold upon the school until a most remarkable revival literally fell upon us and really has never fully subsided. The nightly series finally ceased, but the power and conviction have continued with us. The following account of the wonderful meetings appeared in the papers.

A VERITABLE PENTECOST AT WILMORE, KENTUCKY

I am often pained at the newspaper accounts of revivals written by evangelists and others. In the flush of victory things are penned which seem exaggerations. Everything is in the superlative degree. I wish to record a bit of history concerning a revival now in progress in Asbury College chapel which cannot be exaggerated. The following facts distinguish it and differentiate it from any and all other meetings I have attended in a period of thirty-five years:

(1) It was unannounced, unplanned, unexpected.

(2) The absolute absence of human leadership—everything is spontaneous or, rather, the Spirit guides and directs and nobody leads or knows what is to come next. There is no preaching being done—nobody opens the meeting, nobody has charge and yet services begin and continue and end with salvations, sanctifications and reclamations at every coming together.

(3) Another marked feature is what might be termed the absorption of the meeting. It occupies everybody and about all our wakeful hours. From ten to fifteen hours out of every twenty-four are taken up by the services. Saturday the meeting as usual opened itself, without hymn or prayer or a leader or a word but with shouts and hallelujahs, at 10 a.m., and closed at 11:30 that night. An intermission of an hour and a half for supper was attempted, but the fire fell at the supper table and few ate anything and the supper broke up in a shout.

(4) The emphasis given missions is another feature of this most marvelous display of divine power in our midst. It was preceded by the calling out definitely to the foreign field of a number of our leading young men and young ladies who had long been fighting a battle on this question. Throughout the services, the testimonies, prayers and songs all breathe the holy, fervid love for this sacred cause which lies so near the heart of Asbury. There are more students definitely called and being prepared for foreign mission work in Asbury than ever before. There are probably not less than from forty to fifty. Yesterday after the meeting had run to past noon, and much of the audience had retired, someone called for all who were called to the foreign field to hold up their hands, and thirty-three responded.

(5) I note as the fifth mark of peculiarity in this meeting the unusually profound conviction pervading the assembly. A young man entered the room one night quite drunk and came under immediate conviction, fell at the altar and was converted. One of our professors was walking in the rear of the chapel filled with the Spirit and clapping his hands. He passed a nicely dressed young man and simply asked him if he were a Christian and the young man, without a word, fell on his knees as suddenly as though he had been felled by a rifle shot. The entire chapel is an altar. Not only on front seats are seekers found, but here and there all over the room individuals drop and a few praying friends are seen gathered around each, helping them to victory, and ever and anon above the din of the mighty chorus of joy and triumph from the assembled saints is heard the glad notes of rejoicing of a new-born soul.

(6) The last point is the marvelous demonstrations attendant upon these services. Singularly, at first, those accustomed to shout

were very quiet, and the Spirit fell upon a class of young men and young ladies hitherto wholly undemonstrative. He came upon them in mighty power, producing in them marvelous demonstrations to their own utter surprise and the wonderment of the entire school. Cultured, refined, sedate, dignified young men and young women hitherto absolutely quiet, subdued and reserved in their religious experience, not objecting particularly to demonstration in others, yet in no sense or degree prepossessed in its favor in anybody, but who would certainly have felt personally disgraced to have been found engaged in it, became suddenly and irresistibly possessed of a strange power impelling them to shout, rejoice, clap their hands and in diverse ways give expression to the overflowing ecstasy which thrilled their souls. The young men literally take possession of the house, running, jumping and shouting vociferously. Think of a dozen or two young men of the character I have just described rushing hither and thither laughing and shouting lustily, jumping, clapping hands, rejoicing, embracing each other while as many young ladies of the same class described, on the opposite side of the chapel, have risen to their feet and are clapping their hands, waving handkerchiefs, joyfully laughing and with beautiful voices shouting the praises of God.

After a service or two the power fell upon the veteran shouters who had seemed for a while in a measure restrained. From then on with the veterans and the new recruits combined there have been constantly thrilling scenes and heart-melting sounds which simply beggar descriptions. Not one indecorous thing has yet been done nor indiscreet word uttered. Amid it all salvation work goes on. Amid all this holy recklessness and divine ardor souls seek and find God. Scholarly professors—graduates from our leading universities, men of brains and culture who revel in Greek and Hebrew, philosophy and the sciences—are to be seen in the midst of the boys and girls rejoicing in God and pointing souls to Christ.

I have never seen anything approximating this meeting in any way of the particulars mentioned. It had no beginning, has no leader and needs none, and possesses every feature of a most genuine, phenomenal and divine work of the Holy Spirit. It just came from the Father, breaking out in the Boys' Conference, and the first thing we knew there was a mighty, unprecedented, indescribable, phenomenal, spiritual conflagration among us. I haven't told half the story. It cannot be told in human words. I wish I could portray its grandeur, its glory and its graciousness. The work is not a week old yet. I know not when it will close.

NOTE: A month and a half after the above was written, the following notice by Dr. Haynes appeared in the papers.

AFTERMATH OF THE REVIVAL IN ASBURY COLLEGE. When I say I will write of the "Aftermath of the Great Revival in Asbury College," I am not sure I have correctly stated it. It is more like a continuation of the marvelous meeting of which I wrote your paper a few weeks ago. We got down to regular class work after the regular daily meetings of the revival closed, but the wonderful power of the great revival abides and bursts forth frequently in classroom, chapel, or Boys' Conference or at one of the two daily noonday prayer meetings. Students and teachers who have been here the longest say that they have never seen anything like it before at Asbury. There is the most conscious, and the most continuous and the most wonderful spirit of power and love and faith pervading the institution, flooding hearts, thrilling souls, irradiating faces, and voiced in holy songs, prayers, rapturous shouts and testimonies that I have ever seen prevail anywhere. It is the uniform, distinguishing spirit of the institution. Perpetual triumph is in the air. Joy beams from every face; the divine tenderness, sweetness and love bind the large student body into a beautiful unity. Truly can I say in the language of the beautiful song, "This Is Heaven to Me."

As I write, the halls of the great college building resound with the shouts and rejoicings of the crowd in a recitation room where the noonday prayer meeting is held. We have certainly struck a high-water mark.

[1]*Catalogue of Asbury College for 1906-1907, and Eighteenth Announcement 1907-1908*, pp. 10-14.

WALES, PARADIGM OF A REVIVAL

Students of spontaneous revival will discover a national, even worldwide confluence of outpourings in the years preceding and following the Asbury revivals of 1907, 1935, 1950, 1970, and 1995.

One of the most far-reaching movements of God's Spirit began in Wales in 1904. Yet, few people know about it. One person who sought to fill in the gap was Oxford-educated Dr. J. Edwin Orr. Of him Billy Graham wrote, "Dr. J. Edwin Orr, in my opinion, is one of the greatest authorities on the history of religious revivals in the Protestant world." At the urging of historians Kenneth LaTourette and F.F. Bruce, Orr conducted painstaking academic research on the subject of the Welsh Revival, including how it spread to nations around the world: India, Korea, Norway, Brazil, China, the United States, and more.[1] Fascinating eyewitness accounts from 1905 are available online (the format is cumbersome)[2], or in Kindle edition or used books.[3]

If there is a Welshman whose name stands out it was Evans Roberts. He sought God secretly, humbly, and earnestly with one request, "God, bend me." God heard. Revival came suddenly and unexpectedly. Riveting services that needed no leadership followed. Dusty churches filled to standing room only capacity. Wales was turned upside down with crime almost swept away, reminiscent of Northampton, Massachusetts, as described by Jonathan Edwards in 1735.

In Wales, "One village was so literallly transformed that...swearing was rarely heard. Children met frequently for prayer and even met in school for prayer for revival. 'Even in the granite quarries, workmen are holding prayer meetings of the most impressive character every dinner hour.' ...David Lloyd George, politician and later prime minister, said the effect of the revival was like a tornado sweeping over the nation.... The press in many nations, even Roman Catholic countries like France, Italy, and Portugal, reported the Wales revival extensively and even included photos. Visitors came from [around the world] to see God's power at work.

As time went on, Roberts became more and more convinced of the priority of prayer over all else, even over singing. He said, 'We may sing all night without saving. It is prayer that tells, that saves, and thus brings heaven down among us. Pray, friends, pray.' Roberts did not preach against gambling, dishonesty, drunkenness, injustice, or immorality. He pointed people to Christ the Savior. Yet the social impact of the revival was so very profound, and so many of these sins for a period almost disappeared in Wales."[4]

WALES, PARADIGM OF A REVIVAL, CONTINUED

American publications carried headlines discussing the Welsh Revival. H. C. Morrison's *Pentecostal Herald* raised the question, "WILL GOD COME TO AMERICAN CHURCHES? God has come to Wales. A mighty revival is sweeping that country and thousands are being converted. Will God also come to America?"[5] It was during this time (1905 to 1907) that mention of unusual divine awakenings appear in various publications, including the records of colleges like Asbury and Taylor.

Broadly speaking, some American Christians emphasized the power and presence of the Holy Spirit (Acts 1:8) or spiritual gifts (1 Corinthians 12, Romans 12). Others stressed the character of Christ (Galatians 5:22-23), agape love, and holiness, including Wesleyan views of entire sanctification (Hebrews 12:14). Still others spotlighted the contest for biblical and doctrinal orthodoxy (Jude 1:3, 1 Peter 3:15).

Ideally, these are not mutually exclusive, either-or positions. A key adjective is "conjunctive," a merger of streams toward the unity and fullness of Christ (John 17, Ephesians 4:13-15). As summarized by Timothy Tennent, "Samuel Escobar has wisely stated, Evangelical Protestantism emphasized the 'continuity in truth by the Word,' whereas Pentecostalism has emphasized the 'continuity in life by the Spirit.' To be faithful to Christ in the twenty-first century, the church desperately needs the dynamic union of both."[6]

[1]J. Edwin Orr, *The Flaming Tongue: The Impact of 20th Century Revivals* (Chicago, IL: Moody Press, 1973).

[2]S. B. Shaw, "The Great Revival in Wales," [http://www.theoldtimegospel.org/revival/rev01.html]. accessed 3/31/16.

[3]S. B. Shaw, "The Great Revival in Wales," [http://www.amazon.com/The-Great-Revival-Wales-Shaw-ebook/dp/B00AH8SPW0]. accessed 2/12/16.

[4]Duewel, *Revival Fire*, pp. 198-200.

[5]"Will God Come to America,", *The Pentecostal Herald*, March 1, 1904, p. 2; Thomas Payne, "Talks on the Welsh, and Other Revivals," *Pentecostal Herald*, Wednesday, March 29th, 1905, p. 2.

[6]Timothy C. Tennent, *Invitation to World Missions: A Trinitarian Missiology for the Twenty-first Century* (Grand Rapids, MI: Kregel, Inc.), p. 431.

E. Stanley Jones – 1907*

INTRODUCTION: E. Stanley Jones is one of the most renowned graduates of Asbury College. A world-class missionary and statesman, he was a consultant (even a friend) with leaders like Mahatma Gandhi and President Franklin D. Roosevelt,[1] and he also helped to inspire Reverend Martin Luther King in his efforts for racial justice. The following description is taken from Jones's autobiography, A Song of Ascents.[2]

Since the primary emphases in Asbury were upon "experience" and "expression," it does not seem strange that the two outstanding things that happened to me while at Asbury for four years were in those two realms. There was no attempt to produce those two experiences; they just happened, the most spontaneous, unlooked-for, and unexpected events of my early Christian life. The first seemed sovereignly given, out of a blue sky, without any provocation. Four or five of us students were in the room of another student, Jim Ballinger, having a prayer meeting about ten o'clock at night. I remember I was almost asleep with my head against the bedclothes where I was kneeling, when suddenly we were all swept off our feet by a visitation of the Holy Spirit. We were all filled, flooded by the Spirit. Everything that happened to the disciples on the original Pentecost happened to us. Here I am tempted to tone down what really happened, or to dress it up in garments of respectability by using noncommittal descriptive terms. In either case it would be dishonest or even worse—a betrayal of one of the most sacred and formative gifts of my life, a gift of God. To some who have looked on me as an "intellectual" it will come as a shock. But shock or no shock, here goes. For three or four days it could be said of us as was said of those at the original Pentecost, "They are drunk." I was drunk with God. I say "for three or four days," for time seemed to have lost its significance. The first night I could only walk the floor and praise him. About two o'clock L. L. Pickett, the father of Bishop J. Waskom Pickett, came upstairs and said: "Stanley, he giveth his beloved sleep." But sleep was out of the question. By morning the effects of this sudden and unexpected "outpouring" had begun to go through the college and town. That morning there was no chapel service, in the ordinary sense; people were in prayer, some prostrate in prayer. No one led it, and yet it was led—led by the Spirit. For three days there were no college classes. Every classroom was a prayer meeting where students and faculty were seeking and finding and witnessing. It spread to the countryside. People flocked in, and before they could even get into the assembly hall, would be stricken with conviction and would fall on their knees on the campus crying for God, and pardon and release. I was praying with seekers on the inside of the hall when someone came to me and said: "Come outside. There are people kneeling on the campus who need your help."

And then a strange thing happened: I was taken possession of by an infinite quiet. I found myself tiptoeing as I walked through that auditorium of seeking and rejoicing people. I found myself talking in whispers, the outer expression of this holy calm within. And yet it was a dynamic calm, something akin to the calm at the center of a cyclone—the calm where the dynamic forces of the cyclone reside. It was easy to help people through to victory and release.

When we took stock of what had happened, every single student had professed conversion and apparently had found it, as witnessed by their changed lives, and many from the townspeople and countryside were converted and transformed.

It was the cleanest, the least maneuvered, the most "untouched-by-human-hands," the most constructive and spiritually and morally productive movement I have ever seen. As far as I know, there were no adverse after effects or side effects.

As far as I was concerned, certain things had happened and happened for good and only good: (1) I was released from the fear of emotion. I had tasted three days of ecstasy—drunk with God. And yet they were the clearest-headed, soberest moments I have ever known. I saw into the heart of reality, and the heart of reality was joy, *and love....* (2) At the moment of my highest emotion and ecstasy I was suddenly released from emotion and calm took possession. I had experienced the highest and deepest emotion and yet had been weaned from it in a moment. As I look back, I see that I've never yearned for or desired the return of that or similar emotion. I have Him, and I was nothing besides Him, for in Him there are joy, love, everything. (3) I have said above that "everything that happened to the disciples on the original Pentecost happened to us"—everything except one thing. None of us spoke "in tongues." Why? Certainly God had a chance to give us the gift of tongues if He had wanted to. We were open for anything. Neither in the original group of four or five nor in later manifestations were there any of the "gifts" mentioned or desired. The emphasis was on the gift of the Spirit, instead of on the "gifts of the Spirit"....

(4) As I look back on this experience and ask why this happened at this particular moment of my life, I see it was connected with my choice of my lifework as a missionary. I needed to be prepared personally so he could talk with me about it. I needed to have the inner fetter of an unmentioned sense of superiority that I was here among these rougher and more emotional Kentuckians, and I was from the more cultured and reserved East—needed to have these fetters burned away in the fires of the Spirit. And they were. I had been more emotional than any of them! I had been a fool—now I would be "God's fool." I was free—free from the herd and its superiorities and inferiorities. I was free to be His, with a sort of careless indifference to what people thought. (5) Now He had me in a position where He could talk with me, and I would be disposed to listen. I would be disposed to listen to anything He had to say....But—and this was significant—this experience did not unfit me for the details of life around me. It drove me deeper into them. Life became sacramental. I became a better student. I found myself reading my ordinary so-called secular books kneeling upon my knees. It was secular—it was sacred. The distinction between the secular and sacred had broken down. All life was alive, with God.

(6) But the biggest thing that came out of the experience was my call to the mission field. I had no notion of being a missionary when I went to college....But as I studied the needs of Africa[3] preparing for an address, I became burdened. I knelt down and said: "Now, Lord, I don't want to go into that room to give a missionary address. I want a missionary to go from this meeting, and I'm not going in there until you give me one." He replied: "According to your faith, so be it

unto you." So I arose from my knees and said: "All right, I'll take one."
So the first thing I said to the audience was this: "Somebody is going
to the mission field from this meeting." Little did I know who it would
be, but I was the answer! I had prayed myself into it. Be careful how
you pray; you may be the answer.

*Some sources cite 1905 as the date of this account, but 1907 is
preferred. A contemporary external source is Professor Wray, who
clearly places Jones in the context of 1907.*

[1]E. Stanley Jones, *A Song of Ascents: A Spiritual Autobiography* (Nashville, TN:
Abingdon Press, 1968), pp. 131ff, 200ff. Used by permission, all rights reserved.

[2]Ibid., pp. 68-72.

[3]bid., p. 73. *[NOTE: God routed him to India, not Africa.]*

Dr. Newton Wray – 1907

*INTRODUCTION: Dr. Newton Wray provides an interesting remi-
niscence from his personal experiences while he was a professor at
Asbury. He would also serve as interim president for a short time
(1908-1909). This account appeared in* The Pentecostal Herald *in
1932 as part of a sample from Wray's upcoming autobiography.*[1]

In the fall of 1906 came a call to become a member of the faculty
Asbury College, at Wilmore, Kentucky. At first we had rooms in the
frame dormitory of Asbury, adjacent to the administrative building
which later was the scene of the most wonderful outpouring of the
Holy Spirit I ever witnessed....

During my first three years at Asbury I taught courses in the English
Bible, with Hebrew and Greek New Testament added, Theology,
Christian Evidences and Philosophy. Mrs. Wray taught History.
The third year of my incumbency I was acting president, Dr. B. F. Haynes
having resigned from the presidency to take up work elsewhere....

The second term of my first year at Asbury *[NOTE: recall that Wray
arrived in the Fall of 1906]* was signalized by an extraordinary visitation

of the Holy Spirit. There was no preacher or evangelist to whom it could be in anywise attributed. It began with a small group of students at prayer meeting in one of the classrooms *[NOTE: E. Stanley Jones indicates they were in their lodgings at the home of L. L. Pickett, who boarded students]*, just like the first Pentecost at Jerusalem. It was noised abroad and students came running to see what the uproar was about. The meeting had to be transferred to the chapel. Others were soon drenched with the downpour, and when I stood in their midst, I, too became flooded with tears and hallelujahs. I overheard the remark, "Look at the Professor." There was not leaping, however, on my part; for I have never exhibited emotion in a physical way, unless the Lord was in it. That would only be the flesh working up my excitement. But there was leaping and shouting in a genuine way all over the chapel. Yet, strange as it seemed to some, E. Stanley Jones, to whose mighty, prevailing prayers with those of others, this Pentecost was due, remained silent. I can see him now, sitting on a front seat, quiet, listening, as though he was but a spectator. When asked why he was so quiet and why he was not shouting, he answered that the Lord had not told him to shout. Now Stanley was no pretender. There was and is nothing in him unreal. What the Lord told him to do he would do whatever others might think or not think. Admirable character! No wonder God has used him so mightily on the mission field, and that he could be the author of such books as *The Christ of the Indian Road, Christ at the Round Table*, and *The Christ of Every Road*.

Well, Stanley's time to shout came. It was on a Sunday morning. I was sitting near the front of the church, when suddenly a shout came from the rear as the door opened, and down the aisle Stanley came leaping and shouting, clear into the pulpit where he "prophesied" in the New Testament sense of pouring out truth in the name of the Lord. How long the special meetings went on I do not remember, or how many got saved and were baptized by the Holy Spirit. But that Pentecostal visitation is one of the treasured possessions of my memory and will continue to be while life lasts.

[1]Dr. Newton Wray, "A Teacher in Asbury College," *The Pentecostal Herald*, Nov. 23, 1932, pp. 4-5.

SNAPSHOTS – Changes Big and Small

From Two Campuses to One. Before 1890 Wilmore lacked even a common school, but by September, 1900, it seemed an academic magnet with the opening of a new secondary school. This was Bellevue "College," whose founder and principal was Professor H. T. Boyd. It was located on the west side of North Lexington Avenue. The Asbury campus was on East Main Street. In December, Boyd unaccountably resigned, and by 1905 Bellevue went out of business, leaving several new buildings on the market. Asbury purchased the facilities and divided activities between the two sites. ATL

Rulebook and Policy Updates.

- 1912　The girls' uniforms were modernized to blue jumpers and mortarboard hats.

- 1919　The first meal was served in the new college dining hall. Meals were served "family style" to groups of students assigned to tables. New students were instructed to bring four cloth napkins and a personalized napkin ring when they came to college.

- 1945　The Student-Faculty Committee recommended that motion pictures no longer be classified with smoking, drinking and dancing as expulsion offenses.
The Board agreed.

- 1958　The Board voted to postpone action related to integration. E. Stanley Jones was not sure if he was still on the Board, but he resigned in protest anyway. The tide was changing. New policies were gradually enacted.

- 1969　A rule was introduced that prohibited male students from wearing beards or long hair.

- 1992　Students were allowed beards if they grew them before the school term began. ATL

Diversity. Asbury was one of the first colleges in the world to conduct co-educational learning. The policy was controversial, but Rev. Hughes—having studied the subject for many years—was convinced that there was no better way for "developing a symmetrical character." The school was also one of the most cosmopolitan, drawing students from across the nation. Mary Hughes, John Wesley Hughes's wife, commented on the downside of new students so far from home, i.e. homesickness. By 1931, *The New York Times* reported that the college was second on a list of the ten "most national" colleges in the U.S., along with Yale and other major institutions. It had "the second most ideal distribution of students," from thirty-eight states & eleven foreign countries. ATL.

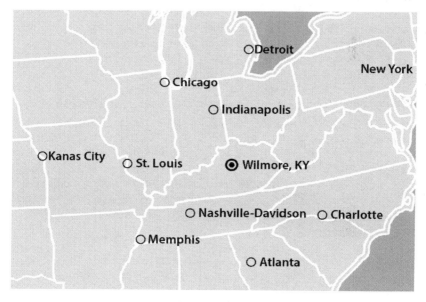

Students were led to Asbury from many places.

WHAT IS SHEKINAH GLORY?

"The term *Shekinah* as commonly used describes the visible manifestation of God's presence and glory usually in the form of a cloud."[1] Visible or not, it refers to the manifest presence of God.

The word is Hebrew in origin. "The word *Shekinah* does not appear in the Bible, but the concept clearly does. The Jewish rabbis coined this extra-biblical expression, a form of a Hebrew word that literally means 'he caused to dwell,' signifying that it was a divine visitation of the presence or dwelling of the Lord God on this earth. The Shekinah was first evident when the Israelites set out from Succoth in their escape from Egypt. There the Lord appeared in a cloudy pillar in the day and a fiery pillar by night (Exodus 13)."[2] During the remainder of the wilderness journey, it is associated with the tabernacle. At later points in the biblical record the manifest presence of God appears—most significantly—at the dedication of Solomon's temple. *"As soon as Solomon finished his prayer, fire came down from heaven and consumed the burnt offering and the sacrifices, and the glory of the LORD filled the temple. And the priests could not enter because the glory of the LORD filled the LORD's house"* (2 Chron. 7:2-3).

The Shekinah cloud of glory dwelling in the Temple has a parallel fulfill-ment in the New Testament. *"The Word became flesh, and dwelt (tab-ernacled) among us, and we beheld His glory, glory as of the Only begotten from the Father, full of grace and truth"* (John 1:14). "In the New Testament, Jesus Christ is the dwelling place of God's glory. Colossians 2:9 tells us that *'in Christ all the fullness of the Deity lives in bodily form,'* and this causes Jesus to say, *'Anyone who has seen me has seen the Father* (John. 14:9).'"[3] To this, the church aspires by grace (Eph. 2-3).

This glory was visibly revealed on the mountain of transfiguration (Mark 9:2-9), later referred to by the apostle Peter in awed tones, *"For when he received honor and glory from God the Father, and the voice was borne to him by the Majestic Glory, 'This is my beloved Son, with whom I am well pleased,' we ourselves heard this very voice borne from heaven, for we were with him on the holy mountain"* (2 Peter 2:16-18). Some scholars believe the Shekinah glory will descend again in Jerusalem and never depart (Ezekiel 43:4-7).

[1] http://www.preceptaustin.org/shekinah_glory.htm (accessed 12/17/16).

[2] http://www.gotquestions.org/shekinah-glory.html (accessed 12/17/16).

[3] Ibid.

BIBLICAL, HISTORICAL, AND THEOLOGICAL FOUNDATIONS

Our Biblical Forebears

Some observers may forget that the unusual accounts in this book have biblical and historical precedents. The focus of this anthology is on "the Lord in the midst of His people," variously described as an outpouring of the Spirit, God drawing near, divine visitation, and so forth.

With few exceptions, the primary focus is *not* on isolated individuals encountering God (sometimes known as a theophany), or having contact with an angel (whether in dreams, visions, or an audible voice). This category would include Abraham, Hagar, Jacob, Joseph, Moses, Isaiah, Daniel, Zachariah, Mary, Stephen, Cornelius, Peter, Paul, Ananias, and John. A second category that is also beyond the scope of this anthology is biblical occurrences that involve God's overruling of the forces of nature, such as physical healings or stilling a storm. Readers interested in a balanced and credible treatment related to acts of God's power (see Hebrews 2:4) may read Dr. Stephen Elliott's book, *By Signs and Wonders: How the Holy Spirit Grows the Church,* Seedbed Press, 2016.

But there are a couple of biblical incidents with distinct parallels to Asbury events. The first involves Solomon's temple in the Old Testament in what is sometimes referred to as Shekinah glory. It was not exactly without antecedents. For instance, the movable tabernacle in the wilderness with its accompanying pillar of cloud and fire was a strong focal point for communal encounters with God. "Moses and Aaron then went into the tent of meeting. When they came out, they blessed the people; and the glory of the LORD appeared to all the people" (Leviticus 9:23). This was Shekinah.

Centuries later Solomon replaced the movable tabernacle with a stationary temple in Jerusalem. At the dedication ceremonies God appeared in a sudden and overwhelming way. "The priests could not enter into the house of the LORD because the glory of the LORD filled the LORD'S house" (2 Chronicles 7:1-2). God was unusually present, and everyone knew it.

In the New Testament, Pentecost deserves particular attention. Beginning forty days after the crucifixion and resurrection of Jesus, a small and fervent group of His followers prayed earnestly for ten solid days. They gathered together on the morning of Pentecost (probably in one of the outer courts of the temple itself), and God moved powerfully among them (Acts 2:1-42). Before the day was over, thousands of people heard the gospel and were baptized. The church was born. A similar episode is described in Acts 4:31, "after they prayed, the place where they were meeting was shaken."

Unlike at Pentecost, outward signs like a mighty wind or speaking in unknown languages were in little evidence at Asbury. But other elements abound. There is deep conviction of sin, confession, and departure from evil. People are transformed. Unity, faith, hope, and love bloom. Vital Christian community is born. Outsiders are drawn inside, insiders go outside. There is an overflow of witness and mission. Above all, the name of Jesus is lifted up and God is glorified (John 12:32).

Case Study from Methodist History

Outside of the Bible, there are similar precedents in Christian history. Though fairly abundant, they are often little known. Christians in the Wesleyan tradition can find vivid examples. The following pages provide a glimpse of the earliest one, what someone has referred to as a Methodist Pentecost.

Starting in 1739, John and Charles Wesley fielded many questions as the British Evangelical Awakening got underway. Around 1735, America's First Great Awakening began in New England. Jonathan Edwards

A METHODIST PENTECOST

JOHN WESLEY – As a leading light of the First Great Awakening and a founder of the Methodist movement, Wesley raised up spiritual heirs numbering over one hundred million worldwide. Below he writes about what we might term a New Year's Watch Night service.

Jan. 1, 1739. Mr. Hall, Kinchin, Ingham, Whitefield, Hutchins, and my brother Charles, were present at our love-feast with sixty of our brethren. About three in the morning, as we were continuing instant in prayer, the power of God came mightily upon us, insomuch that many cried out for exceeding joy, and many fell to the ground. As soon as we were recovered a little from that awe and amazement at the presence of his majesty, we broke out with one voice, "We praise thee, O God, we acknowledge thee to be the Lord."[1] [The Latin "Te Deum" in the 1662 *Book of Common Prayer*].

GEORGE WHITEFIELD – He was arguably the most well-known preacher of the eighteenth Century. His friend and admirer, Benjamin Franklin, estimated that Whitefield could be heard by crowds of up to thirty thousand people... without a microphone! Here is Whitefield's description of the same New Year's service and the aftermath.

Jan. 1, 1739. I found this to be the happiest New Year's Day that I ever yet saw. Oh! What mercies has the Lord shown me since this time twelve months ago! And yet I shall see greater things than these. Oh that my heart may be prepared.

Jan 5, 1739. Held a Conference at Islington, concerning several things of very great importance, with seven true ministers of Jesus Christ, despised Methodists, whom God has brought together....We continued in fasting and prayer 'till three o'clock, and then parted with a full conviction that God was going to do great things among us.[2]

CONCLUSION: Within four months a spiritual movement exploded. These "despised" Methodists took the good news of Jesus Christ outside church doors to fields and factories, to desperate people bent by misery or bound by indifference. The movement began in England and skipped overseas to the British colonial empire, where it impacted—no, more than impacted—where it transformed the world.

[1]John Wesley, *Wesley's Works, 3rd Edition, Volume I,* Thomas Jackson, editor (Grand Rapids, MI: Baker Book House, 1978), p. 170.

[2]George Whitefield, *Reverend Mr. George Whitefield's Journal from his Arrival at London, to his departure from thence on his way to Georgia, 1739, 3rd Journal Edition* (James Hutton, Bible and Sun, without Temple-Bar.17). http://quintapress.macmate.me/PDF_Books/Third_Journal_Text_v2.pdf (accessed 12/13/16).

(a talented pastor, theologian, and writer who later served as the third president of Princeton University) was an astonished witness. Edwards recorded his observations,[1] which served as an inspiration and practical guide to George Whitefield and John Wesley... but not without controversy.

Barred from Epworth church, Wesley speaks from his father's grave, 1742.

In Defense of "Enthusiasm"

At the very onset of the revival the Wesley brothers were called on the carpet (literally in one instance) by two Anglican bishops who criticized the Methodist movement over seeming irregularities (theological, experiential, and administrative). Huge crowds of mainly middle and poorer working-class people were gathering outdoors in all kinds of weather to hear them speak. Untrained lay preachers, dubbed "circuit riders," took up the mantle, traveling about preaching the gospel with little respect for parish boundaries. People were finding God and were unwilling to hide the news under a bushel. These experiences attracted some negative attention. One criticism was "enthusiasm" (from Latin, "inspired by a deity"), which at the time meant a form of religious madness, conjuring images associated with the social chaos of the English Civil Wars (1642–1651).

Wesley sought to turn the tables on these detractors. He countered that enthusiasm—in the negative sense of the word—emerges when people think they enjoy grace but don't, or when they fail to grasp the difference between nominal and real Christianity. "Talk of righteousness and peace and joy in the Holy Ghost," he pointed out, and such detractors will conclude, "Thou art beside thyself."[2]

Generally speaking, Asbury revivals are notable for a certain degree of decorum. Nevertheless, some descriptions are thick with emotion. Understandably, strong emotion may repel or create discomfort in people who are reserved by temperament or who by upbringing are inclined toward modesty, order, and less public display of feelings. However, the temptation to omit some portions of these accounts would involve burying historical records to suit some tastes.

Besides, displays of emotion do not necessarily discount the reality of God's presence. They may even reinforce the argument. Undoubtedly God may be present with us whether we *feel* anything or not. In Matt. 18:20 we read Christ's promise, "Wherever two or three gather together in my name, there am I with them." But when an angel actually appears in Scripture, people typically bow down in awesome wonder. They take their shoes off.

It took years for the Methodist movement to gain widespread respect. In the meantime, the principal leaders were unwilling to be cowed by accusations of "enthusiasm." After all, what did the apostles do at Pentecost when some mocking bystanders said, "These men are drunk with new wine"? Peter called attention to Scripture and said, "This is God's doing, foretold long ago" (Acts 2:16).

Events came to a head in 1744 at St. Mary's, Oxford. John Wesley had been an Oxford Fellow, studied seven languages, and was a master of logic and debate. He addressed the critics directly in a well-intentioned but bold message; the place was jammed with faculty and students. His sermon was entitled "Scriptural Christianity."

> May it not be.... so many of you are a generation of *triflers*; triflers with God, with one another, and with your own souls? For how many of you spend, from one week to another, a single hour in private prayer? How few have any thought of God in the general tenor of your conversation? Who of you is in any degree acquainted with the work of His Spirit? His supernatural work in the souls of men? Can you bear, unless now and then in a church, any talk of the Holy Ghost? Would you not take it for granted if one began such a conversation that it was either "hypocrisy" or "enthusiasm"? In the name of the Lord God Almighty I ask, What religion are you of? Even the talk of Christianity ye cannot, will not, bear! O my brethren! What a Christian city is this? "It is time for thee, Lord to lay to thine hand!".... Lord, save or we perish![3]

How did the listeners respond? Some were touched. But the official reaction was this: tenured or not, it was John Wesley's final sermon at Oxford University. He was never invited to speak there again.

Meanwhile, the revival swelled in size and influence; it eventually gave birth to scores of church bodies and movements throughout history, ironically including some reinvigoration of the Anglican Church of which Wesley was a member. It was a fresh version of God's new song, a revival, a gift from God.

Many Eventually Come Around

Recently I was driving with my son, Jonathan, an Anglican priest. We listened to an exquisite Twila Paris recording of Charles Wesley's song, "Arise My Soul Arise."

> Arise, my soul arise; shake off thy guilty fears,
> The bleeding sacrifice, on my behalf appears;
> Before the throne my surety stands,
> Before the throne my surety stands:
> My name is written on His hands.
>
> Five bleeding wounds He bears, received on Calvary;
> They pour effectual prayers, they strongly plead for me:
> Forgive him, Oh, forgive they cry!
> Forgive him, Oh, forgive they cry!
> Nor let that ransomed sinner die.
>
> My God is reconciled, His pardoning voice I hear;
> He owns me for His child, I can no longer fear:
> With confidence I now draw nigh;
> With confidence I now draw nigh,
> And Father, Abba*, Father! cry.
>
> *Abba is akin to our "Daddy."

I turned and said, "Jonathan, those lyrics came from the heart of Charles Wesley, arguably the finest Anglican hymn writer of all time." Jonathan replied, "You are probably right." Incidentally, John and Charles Wesley are now acknowledged on May 24 in the Church of England Calendar of Saints. Initial distaste eventually transitioned into final embrace because the outward trappings receded in light of the heavenly glory.

Theological Reflection

One question worth probing is, "Why did God come in this way and at these times?" There are hints in three words: 1) orthodoxy (right thinking), 2) orthopraxy (right living), and a newer word, 3) orthopathy (right feeling). These three correspond to mind, will, and emotion, or—if you will—head, hands, and heart. Believers need all three. Orthodoxy without the other two becomes arid doctrine. Orthopraxy without the other two tends toward rigid legalism. Orthopathy without the others veers toward sentimentality or fanaticism. In spontaneous revival, God seems to show up personally, not actually incarnate, yet a Jesus we can almost touch (1 John 1:1).[4] Head, heart, and hands come alive, but especially the heart. This is particularly needed in an age of rationalism and pragmatism. When Paul wrote the Ephesian epistle, he prayed that "the eyes of your hearts may be enlightened" (Ephesians 1:18). Like Peter, James, and John on the mountain of Transfiguration (Mark 9, 1 Peter 1), witnesses in this anthology appear to have glimpsed something that was both life-changing... and hard to forget.

What can we make of all this? To its credit, Asbury has apparently kept the welcome mat out for somewhat unusual visitations by God. Perhaps God shows up because Asburians expect it and prepare accordingly. I suspect this stems in part from the Wesleyan Arminian theological tradition with its conceptual understanding of the stages of grace.

These stages of grace (otherwise known as the *Via Salutis* or way of salvation) are:

1) PREVENIENT - Prevenient grace occurs before a person even comes to Christ; God is at work drawing them home (Luke 15:11ff, Revelation 3:20).

2) JUSTIFIYING - Justification by grace through faith occurs when a person consciously believes and is saved from the guilt of sin, restored to divine favor, and regenerated, i.e. born again (Eph. 2:8-9, Jn. 3:3).

3) ASSURANCE - The inward witness of the Holy Spirit assures believers

that they are children of God. This is a birthright that should be claimed by every child of God (John 5:24, Romans 8:15, Galatians 4:6).

4) SANCTIFYING - God's continuing work—both progressive and instantaneous—to save from the power and root of sin, and restore the divine image (θέωσις , *theosis*, Christ became what we are so we could become like Him) with a pronounced emphasis on agape love (Romans 8:29, 2 Peter 3:14, 1 John 3:1-3).

5) GLORIFYING - God finishes the work at our death or at Christ's final appearing, which will include restoration of planet earth and creation itself to divine purposes (Romans 8:19-34, Revelation 21).

It is good to stay humble, to hunger and thirst for God, and to keep an open mind and an open heart. No doubt there will be surprises when the Lord comes in manifest presence and power.

[1] Jonathan Edwards, *A Faithful Narrative of the Surprising Work of God in the Conversion of Many Hundred Souls in Northampton and the Neighboring Towns and Villages of New Hampshire, in New England*, 1737. Digital at www.ccel.org/edwards/works1.vii.html (accessed 12/13/16).

[2] John Wesley, "The Nature of Enthusiasm," *The Sermons of John Wesley: A Collection for the Christian Journey*, Kenneth J. Collins and Jason E. Vickers, eds. (Nashville, TN: Abingdon Press, 2013), p. 214.

[3] John Wesley, "Scriptural Christianity," *The Sermons of John Wesley: A Collection for the Christian Journey,* Kenneth J. Collins and Jason E. Vickers, eds. (Nashville, TN: Abingdon Press, 2013), p. 214.

[4] Jonathan Raymond, *Higher Higher Education* (Spring Valley, CA: Aldersgate Press, 2015), p. 9.

NOTE: Page 24. Illustration Biblical scene of Pentecost Image ID:336154817, Copyright: Bernardo Ramonfaur. Used by permission.

SNAPSHOTS – Growth Brings Change

Students. When Asbury first opened, students of all ages were invited. As in many liberal arts colleges of the era, Hughes intended to offer instruction on the elementary, secondary and collegiate levels in at Asbury. At the time the town lacked an elementary and secondary school. The high school was renamed Bethel Academy in 1920; the parting of the schools occurred over time in the wake of changing customs and standards of accreditation. Asbury Seminary, launched in 1923, formally separated in 1939. ATL.

Enrollment. Classes began on September 2, 1890, with eleven students and three teachers. College enrollment grew to 526 by 1940, 1,135 by 1967, and stood at 1,764 in 2012. ATL.

Mottos and Foundational Statements

1740   Singleness of Intention and Purity of Affection—*John Wesley, c. 1730.*

1741   To reform the nation and spread scriptural holiness across the land—*John Wesley.*

1891   First Official Seal: Side A, "Holiness to the Lord"; Side B, "Industry, Thoroughness, Salvation."

1916   Fear God and Work Hard.

1925   Eruditio et Religio (i.e. In Latin, Scholarship and Religion)— *Lewis R. Akers.*

1928   Free salvation for all men; full salvation from all sin (1st of two stone captions, here and below, Hughes Chapel).

1928   Pursue peace with all men, and holiness without which no one shall see the Lord (Heb. 12:14).

1996   Academic Excellence & Spiritual Vitality—*David Gyertson.* ATL

William Pryde Gillis – 1908

INTRODUCTION: The outpouring of 1907 was characterized by a spirit of rejoicing. In 1908 circumstances took a somewhat different direction characterized by a "spirit of intercessory prayer." Graduating senior W.P. Gillis wrote this description, which was included in the official Asbury College Catalogue.[1]

Last year Asbury College was visited with a most phenomenal Pentecostal revival. Like a thunderbolt from a clear sky, it broke upon us, and for about two weeks the college was the theater of indescribable scenes in which students were saved or sanctified or called to the foreign mission field.

It is a remarkable coincidence that at about the same time, and in almost the same manner, a revival has just visited us which in many respects is the exact counterpart of the memorable one of last year.

Like its antecedent of last year, it was unannounced and wholly unplanned. The absence of any regularly appointed human leader is another point of similarity. The Holy Spirit was the chief executive and everyone acted as He dictated. The service lasted from morning until almost midnight, with only some slight intermission for meals or a short rest. Almost every hour of the day sinners were seeking God, and ever and anon glad shouts and hallelujahs of new-born souls rose above the din of prayer.

In the chapel service on the morning of February 18 someone was asked to lead in prayer. In a few minutes the spirit of intercession fell upon us, and it seemed that the very heavens would be rent by the agonizing, importunate cries of young men and women. An altar call was given, and one young man, trembling with conviction, came forward to seek God. Then the Christians again gave themselves to prayer. Such praying that followed beggars description.

The revival was sustained by prayer. Last year the notable characteristic of the revival was the spirit of praise. This year, while the joy of the Lord has been wonderfully upon us, yet the energy has been mostly expended in agonizing prayer. As the prayers waxed fervent, the power of God fell with redoubled force. It was indeed a prayed down revival.

The spirit of prayer was not only intense; it was practically incessant. One student prayed all night. The faculty had a daily prayer meeting in the afternoon. Half an hour after breakfast the boys gathered in the various dormitories and prayed until chapel time (8:15 a.m.). Then again in chapel, prayer would break out with such uncontrollable vehemence that it was almost irresistible. It reminded me of some of the experiences I have read concerning Charles G. Finney and of the great services of the 1850s.

The pungent conviction that prevailed was remarkable. Some very desperate cases were reached. One young man insisted that he did not want to be saved. "I want to go to hell," he said. He was struck with conviction and soon converted, then later sanctified, and is now rejoicing in a call to the mission field. With a despairing wail, one young man cried out. "I am lost, I am lost. Oh, what shall I do?"

The messages given at night by the students were generally on sin and the certainty of the judgment; and surely we had judgment-day conviction. It was a time of great heart-searching among Christians. Many confessions, both public and private, were made. Letters were written, explanations made, sins confessed and wrongs righted.

The revival spirit is still with us and a higher spiritual life prevails. Many have learned the secret of prevailing prayer, and the faith of all has been strengthened. The Boys' Conference has just closed a two-week rally on missions. Several students have been called to the foreign field; many are honestly considering the question and the general interest in missions has increased.

The revival has been an incalculable blessing to me. Before the year closes I hope to be preaching Christ to the [Muslims] of North Africa. I realize that I am now better prepared to meet these implacable foes of the cross by having been in the revival. The possibilities of prayer have been impressed upon me as never before. I am profoundly grateful to God for the institution in which such revivals as this are possible, and though I shall soon bid adieu to these scenes, I shall ever carry with me the tender memories of five years spent in the sacred halls of Asbury.

W. P. Gillies [sic], Student

[1]*Catalogue of Asbury College for 1907-1908 and Annual Announcement for 1908-1909*, pp. 10-11.

Henry Clay Morrison – 1910

INTRODUCTION: Like John Wesley Hughes, Henry C. Morrison is included in these pages because his personal experiences of God's unfathomable grace represent the general Wesleyan ethos that set the stage for revivals. I am dating this inclusion based on the year he assumed the presidency, but his involvement begins in 1890. As such, he is a founding father. Some extended background is in order.

More than any other person, Morrison kept Asbury College alive and thriving during the first fifty years of its existence. In 1889 he assumed the editorship of a small struggling publication, The Old Methodist. *He soon renamed it* The Pentecostal Herald, *a name that he refused to relinquish in later years in spite of its associations with what would become classic Pentecostalism because, as he put it, "The Lord gave us that name." He transformed the* Herald *into a highly successful national publication and from its inauguration continually promoted Asbury through its pages. Time and again the subscribers prayed and gave supplemental donations to help keep Asbury afloat during lean years.*

The Trustees twice called Morrison to serve as president, from 1910 to 1925 when they basically said, "We see no other choice, either you serve or we will have to close the college," and from 1933 to 1940. Amid these two terms he founded Asbury Theological Seminary, unofficially in 1923, officially in 1926, serving as its first president from its inception until his death in 1942. The seminary was originally housed in the building that still bears his name, "Morrison Hall."

Referred to by some as a "benevolent dictator," in later years he cut an illustrious figure with long white locks and flowing Prince

Albert coat, like someone cut out of a Currier and Ives era lithograph. But he was anything but fake. For example, with the college often pressed for funds, Morrison refused a salary for the first several years of his presidency, inspiring the invariably underpaid staff as well as donors.

We can only imagine how he managed throughout these years to conduct a heavy evangelistic and preaching ministry on a national and global basis. Morrison was described as the greatest orator in America during his lifetime, and Dr. Dennis Kinlaw referred to his message "The Offering of Isaac," as the most moving sermon he ever heard.

He was a daring and adventurous leader from his earliest years of ministry, when he started out as a "circuit walker" (without a horse he said he couldn't be called a circuit rider).

One day during some meetings, when [Henry Clay Morrison was] dining with friends on the banks of the Ohio, the question came up as to the ability of anyone present to swim the river, whereupon young Morrison announced that he could swim it. All the company dared him to undertake it; backing down did not belong to his make-up, and he bravely ordered them to follow him in a boat, in case his strength should fail. To the astonishment of all, he swam to the Indiana shore without assistance of the boat. A year later, when serving the Concord Charge, the young men who knew something of his reputation as a swimmer said he could not swim the Ohio River, as he publicly stated that he could...This time the current was swift and he was borne far down the river, but he finally reached the Hoosier side, exhausted, but victorious. "This feat," he declared, "did not hurt the size of my congregation the next Sunday."[1]

Not easily intimidated, he stirred up the entire Methodist Episcopal Church, South, by his refusal to leave Dublin, Texas, where he was leading outdoor services in 1896. The real bone of contention was the Wesleyan doctrine of entire sanctification, and although the local pastor could find nothing to disparage in regard to Morrison's character or overall doctrine, he nevertheless launched a trial to bar Morrison from preaching in his parish. Meanwhile, crowds swelled to standing room only proportions at the outdoor services. I cannot help thinking about John Wesley preaching from his father's tombstone or declaring, "The world is my parish" when criticized for field preaching.

The incident reached General Conference and became known as "The Morrison Case." It is a complex saga.[2] Morrison lost his preaching credentials, only to have them reinstated. Then, to circumvent a new ecclesiastical law, he temporarily withdrew his membership from the church in 1898, but continued to preach as an independent evangelist. By the end of his life he was eventually invited as the guest speaker to more Methodist Annual Conferences (both North and South) than almost any other man living.

This final story occurred early in his ministry. It provides a glimpse into his initial experience of what John Wesley called "The Grand Depositum" of Methodism, i.e. entire sanctification or perfect love. His subsequent experiences pass Wesley's tests for genuineness. They are not religious madness, chiefly because they are attested by scripture, arise from a keenly rational mind and a sound temperament, and eventuate in Christian love.[2] At first Morrison doubted the classical doctrine of holiness, which many prominent segments of American Methodism were abandoning as part of their "pilgrimage to respectability,"[3] or in the reconstruction era south due to its purported associations with Phoebe Palmer and the northern Methodist Church.[4] Nevertheless, the testimony of others convinced him otherwise, particularly a letter from his friend Horace Cockrill who referred him to John Wesley's sermon, A Plain Account of Christian Perfection. *Here is Morrison's account.*

The truth broke in upon me like an inspiration; I saw the doctrine and experience of full salvation as clearly as the sun in a cloudless noonday sky. My whole heart said, "It is the truth," and I laughed and wept for joy. It seemed as if the following conversation went on in my breast: "I am the Lord's child. Yes but not his holy child. He wants me to be holy, but I cannot make myself holy. That is so, but he can make me holy." "Yes, he can," was the response of my whole heart. I saw clearly the reasonableness of it all, and the will and power of God in the matter. I felt assured that I should return to my boarding house after dinner, go to my room, and receive the blessing as a free gift to God."

When Morrison arrived at his room, his friend, Dr. H. C. Young, suggested it was a good idea to end his revival meetings, for there were few prospects of having a genuine revival. This was so contrary to Morrison's appraisal of the possibility of a spiritual awakening that he remonstrated with the friend. Morrison graphically described the subsequent scene.

"Why, Doctor," said I, "the power of God is all over this hill." Throwing up my hands, I said, "the power of God is all over this room. I feel it now." Instantly, the Spirit fell on me and I fell backward on a divan, as helpless as a dead man. I was conscious of the mighty hand of God dealing with me. Dr. Young leaped up, called me again and again, but I was powerless to answer.

Just as I came to myself and recovered the use of my limbs, a round ball of liquid fire seemed to strike me in the face, dissolve, and enter into me. I leaped up and shouted aloud, "Glory to God!" Dr. Young, who still had me in his arms, threw me back on the divan and said, "Morrison, what do you mean? You frightened me. I thought you were dying. Why did you act that way?" "I did not do anything, Doctor," I said, "the Lord did it." I rose and walked the floor, feeling as light as a feather.[5]

CONCLUSION: These seemingly foreign and archaic descriptions come from the pen of a founding father. Could this partly explain why he moved to Wilmore in the wake of the 1907 revival? He wanted to live close to the place of divine visitation. With a call to nonstop itinerant ministry, H. C. Morrison had scant opportunity to stay at home, but who can blame him for wanting— like the apostle Peter—to build a tabernacle on the mountain, even if his time for unbroken heavenly rapture was premature?

[1]C. F. Wimberly, *A Biographical Sketch of Henry Clay Morrison, D.D., Editor of the 'Pentecostal Herald'* (New York and Chicago: Fleming H. Revell Co., 1922), p. 80.

[2]Percival A. Wesche, *Henry Clay Morrison, "Crusader Saint,"* 40th Anniversary Committee Edition (Wilmore, KY: Asbury Theological Seminary, 1963), pp. 82-92.

[3]*The Sermons of John Wesley: A Collection for the Christian Journey*, Kenneth J. Collins and Jason E. Vickers, eds. (Nashville: Abingdon Press, 2014), pp. 214-223.

[4]Randall J. Stephens, "The Holiness, Pentecostal, Charismatic Extension of the Wesleyan Tradition," *The Cambridge Companion to John Wesley,* Randy L. Maddox and Jason E. Vickers, eds. (New York: Cambridge University Press, 2010), p. 265.

[5]J. Lawrence Brasher, *The Sanctified South: John Lakin Brasher and the Holiness Movement* (Urbana and Chicago: University of Illinois Press, 1994), p. 50.

[6]Percival A. Wesche, *Henry Clay Morrison, "Crusader Saint,"* pp. 42-44.

New Era College Reporter – 1916[1]

INTRODUCTION: Reading between the lines, the "College Reporter" is a student eyewitness who did some homework. Although there were hidden roots of prayer, the revival itself began among students and then spread until the entire college became illuminated with spiritual fire. The author is at a loss to fully describe it. Participants were showered with divine peace, cleansing grace, and propulsion toward ministry. There was a general absence of human orchestration amid an atmosphere of decency and order. There is a historical reference to another revival which started years earlier in another Boys' Conference (no doubt in 1908).

The article was written several days into the revival but before it ended. As was often the case, President H. C. Morrison was engaged elsewhere. These were trying times for the college and the world. Morrison took fresh encouragement when he heard the reports. God was among them; what had they to fear?

Spontaneous Revival in Asbury

Should we say spontaneous? Probably not. It is seldom that God does a mighty work for a people without some cause back of it, some human instrumentality intervening. It is customary in these times to make much of preparation in the way of an evangelist, much outward exhortation and human influence.

The Boys' Conference in Asbury has been called the "coaling station" for the school. It is true that much of the propelling power to keep the old ship of real vital Christian life moving onward through the nine months is received in the devotional meetings of this organization.

It was on the evening of March 3, during a testimony meeting in this assembly, that the revival of which we are speaking broke out, and everyone present felt a special manifestation of the mighty power of the Spirit.

Those present left that evening with a feeling that God wanted to send a revival. There was a problem in the minds of many. The winter term examinations were right on, and all felt inclined to do extra study in preparation for the same, but there was a general submission to God's will, and all said with one accord, faculty and students, "Let God do His work in His own good time." The general opinion is that if God is in the heart, lessons will be pursued more easily. The best student is the Christian student.

On the second evening after a short exhortation by one of the boys of the conference, some came and bowed at an altar of prayer. There was one bright conversion. Everyone seemed led on and drawn out to let the Lord come and do His mighty work.

The next day was the Sabbath. By this time the girls of the school, as well as the faculty, had become interested and were attending the meetings. In the afternoon Brother Huston, one of the men of the conference, brought us a real vital message on faith. The Spirit of the Lord was upon him and he preached with liberty and convincing power. This was a great meeting because His Spirit was present and reanointed many of the people of God.

On Monday and Tuesday evenings Miss Nevitt, one of our most loved lady teachers, brought two stirring messages. There was a softening up, a breaking down, a searching out, a general inventory on the part of every Christian. If there ever was a time that people saw themselves in a mirror it was at these meetings. Miss Nevitt's clear testimony of her complete deliverance from the carnal nature and all of the evils which accompany it made those who were not filled with the Holy Spirit long for Him and started them on a search for that experience. The reason for the success of these meetings was that the leader was filled with perfect love and she moved as the Spirit moved her.

Wednesday evening, Professor Larabee had charge of the service. I say had charge of the service, because it was getting to the place where preaching was not necessary. The Holy Ghost seemed to take charge and lead, and when He leads, things are done in the right way, in the decency and order of which Paul speaks. The Spirit did great and mighty work in this meeting in the cleansing of believers and the refreshing of the saints.

We feel that the human should be in the background in this report because it is so in the meeting. From this time on the appointed leader seemed to have no more part in the services than the people of the congregation. Just as in a family discussion of what was needed from God, each one who felt that the Lord was impressing them to say something would arise and deliver his or her soul. This has been carried on to the present. In the last six years that we have been in the school we feel that we have never seen such a manifestation of power. Never have the people been freer to speak the sentiment of their hearts, and for this reason the testimonies have been showers of softening rain. As a general thing in revival work there seems to be a tendency on the part of the people to confess frankly and honestly their state of grace. There seems to be no dread of criticism if they were impressed to go to the altar. In this meeting this has been the case. Everyone seems to be in sympathy. There is a feeling that the Holy Ghost is doing this work, and that it will last. Now we are just on the verge of what we feel this meeting is going to be. One of the noticeable characteristics is the extra quality of faith. There seems to be an assurance of greater things ahead. This faith in God has taken out that human strain and uneasiness which often accompanies such work.

Once before, several years ago, a revival of the same nature broke out in the same organization. We understand that there was much prayer on the part of a few for that revival. After investigation we find that two or three young men have been praying earnestly for two or three weeks for the Lord to visit the Boys' Conference in a mighty awakening. There can always be found back of great spiritual work a waiting people, a soul interceding. God answers prayer. The reward of these young men will no doubt be great because it will mean much to the school, and no one knows the blessing it will be to the world. No doubt some will be called into the ministry and mission field who probably will win thousands of souls for the Master. Those who are preparing for the ministry will receive an impetus and power which will make their lives more fruitful. We hope the reader will get some faint idea of what the Lord is doing for us. You can't feel what we feel. You can only get an idea of the glorious work that is being done. We expect to be able to tell you of greater things later.

[1]"Spontaneous Revival in Asbury," *Asbury College New Era*, March 21, 1916, Vol. 2 No 1, pp. 1-2.

SNAPSHOTS – Before and After

What Students Must Do to Stay in School. In 1908 the passing average was lowered from 80% to 75%. In 2016 many old timers look at Asbury's present academic standards and think, "As things stand now, I couldn't get in." Students in 2016 see the traditional dress and dating standards and think, "Given the guidelines back then, I wouldn't want to get in." ATL.

Ministerial Training in World War One. Many changes occurred in 1917. Enrollment was 416 and of these, 160 were studying for the ministry or mission field. The "Boys' Conference" was renamed "Ministerial Association." The format based on Methodist Conference activity was dropped, and a new schedule of weekly meetings with outside speakers adopted. When the U.S. declared war in April 1917, ministerial exemptions did not cover the majority of men. Many, including some with exemptions, enlisted. Many others left school to take high-paying jobs in war industries. ATL.

Let There Be Light. On March 28, 1925, the Senior Class dedicated their Class gift, a new elevated metal water tank behind Wesley Hall.

The entire Class, in cap and gown, with the faculty and the college band, led the student body from chapel to the site, for an impressive ceremony. The band was on duty again when, at last, Asbury was connected by a special overland line to the Kentucky Utilities Company power plant. The era of kerosene lamps, gas lighting and the free-standing one-horse generator was over. The campus celebrated with band music, singing, and cheering. "It was like a revival meeting. There was light." ATL.

John Paul – 1921

INTRODUCTION: John Paul was Vice President of Asbury College when he penned this account. Paul described the revival as a "dynamo that shocked them out of earth into glory." Throughout the preceding fall term, intercessory prayer went on for this revival, which (like many others) burst forth in February.

PENTECOST AT ASBURY COLLEGE, by John Paul.[1] This is an imposing title, but those who witnessed the ground swell of convicting grace and the sweep of converting and sanctifying power in the February revival in Asbury College can think of no better word to express it. If the passion of prayer, the solicitude for souls and the royal anointings of the Spirit can be perpetuated in the fields where Asbury students and teachers will be laboring in the tomorrows, then will be fulfilled the only other essential mark of Pentecost.

The wholesome features of the visitation were: (1) Prayer as a main factor. (2) The absence of spell-binding or dramatic appeal. (3) Clear instruction and definite emphasis upon Scriptural truth. (4) The absence of any disposition to look for material phenomena or physical miracle, or to point to these as necessary requisites in a soul-saving revival. (5) Spontaneous movement in altar calls, altar work, testimony, and even in the evangelistic offering. (6) The salvation of almost every soul, in every dormitory, and a bright profession of sanctification from many who were not converted till this meeting. An expressed hunger for holiness was universal, where the blessing was not realized.

As we now reflect, it appears that the signs of foundation work began with the day of prayer at the opening of the financial campaign in the fall; and, although the holidays brought their usual unspiritual influence, the advance was steady from the first days of January. Rev. C. W. Butler of Detroit was chosen to do the preaching for the special days; and as he gave line upon line of the plainest kind of gospel truth, with much definite preaching on sanctification, conviction increased like magic. Each altar call was easier than the one preceding, and the employment of invitation songs and propositions to manipulate the unsaved were almost unknown in the meeting. Sometimes a sufficient number of souls to crowd the altar would rise as a unit when the signal was given. Although there was much physical fatigue, soon there was little regard for slumber, and with many, little thought of meal time. On Brother Butler's last night with us, the altar service swept on till six o'clock in the morning. We ran three days longer under the leadership of Dr. W. E. Harrison, a member of the faculty, excepting that I preached the eleven o'clock sermon on Sunday. In the first service, Friday morning, there were scenes beyond all description. The coming to the altar seemed to strike a dynamo that literally shocked them out of earth into glory. To them that did not come to the altar the altar was taken; and, most of the day, on main floor and balcony, circles of prayer were seen around unsaved or unsanctified souls, punctuated with occasional victories. And how they did come through! Asbury is not usually a noisy place in its religious life, but the kind of blessing that most people got in this meeting seemed to take them beyond themselves. Through that Friday, till late in the night, special baptisms were falling upon the most staid and quiet saints, till they were surprised at their own conduct. The altar service that evening was marvelous for the spontaneity of its results, in people who had made no move previous to this meeting. One young man hurried down the aisle for the altar and stopped to tell me there was no use to go, for he had got the blessing of sanctification on the way. He went to the platform instead of the altar. The sudden conversion or sanctification of souls as they arrived at the altar produced a sensation equal to a charge in battle. All day Saturday there was little chance for anything but the work of the meeting. Sunday morning in the church with which the college worships on the Sabbath there was salvation at the altar, among the community people, and it was announced that the meetings had just about made a clean sweep in the dormitories. The Sunday night service, with which the special series closed, was one of decided victory.

If we may have wisdom to conserve the work against the loss that usually follows great revivals, and to stimulate our large group of preachers and missionaries as they go forth, to build according to the vision God has shown them in the mount, the blessing that has recently fallen upon Asbury College will have fallen upon continents, rather than upon a bluegrass village.

NOTE: As a footnote, the move of God's Spirit in 1921 apparently began among students even though there was the traditional element of a guest speaker. The following student news story predates the account by John Paul.[2]

Again we thank the Lord for this gracious revival season He has permitted to come into our school. It was truly sent down from above. On the evening of January 24, in the Boys' Conference, the Lord blessed wonderfully. So the revival truly started before the evangelist, Dr. Butler of Detroit, Michigan, who conducted the services, came on January 25. He was able to be with us only ten days, so we threw ourselves into the meeting with greater effort than usual. We thank the Lord for such men as Dr. Butler, who lives so close to the Lord that He spoke through him such clear and instructive message of full and free salvation that the way to Christ and living in him was made plain.

[1]John Paul, "Pentecost at Asbury College," *Asbury College New Era,* Vol. 7, March 1, 1921, pp. 1, 5.

[2]*"News Department,"* Roy Ruth, ed., with Jeannie Garvey, assistant ed., *Asbury College New Era, Vol. 7, No. 11, p. 6, Feb. 15, 1921.*

Lela McConnell – 1921

INTRODUCTION: Dr. Z. T. Johnson, a former graduate and long-time president of Asbury, indicates in his personal records that Lela McConnell participated in the Revival of 1921, describing it as an unusually powerful one,[1] and something that lingered in her memory.[2] I have tried to substantiate this possibility, but school records and her autobiographical material indicate she did not arrive at Asbury until 1922 when she was thirty-eight years old. What may we conclude? Perhaps her autobiographical timeline is slightly off, or she visited the school during 1921, or participated in another Asbury revival that included Rev. Butler, or the school was basking in the wake of the 1921 revival and she was describing the effects. Whatever the case, another earlier Asbury revival is connected to Lela's story, even if 1921 is somewhat cloudy.

In 1915 a young ministerial student, Ozias Claude Mingledorff (1918), founded the Mountain Missionary Society. He participated in the Boys' Conference (later renamed the Ministerial Association) revival that same school year. This campus society was a springboard for Lela McConnell's journey to the mountains. There she would launch Mt. Carmel High School and the Kentucky Mountain Bible Institute, fondly referred to as "Baby Asbury." One gets a sense of how the spiritual atmosphere at Asbury overflowed in mission and service.

Lela's earliest years are full of colorful adventure, and I refer the reader to her inspiring autobiography, the source of the adapted material provided below.[3] The story begins in the year 1918, a couple of years before she came to Asbury. In particular, it highlights the lasting legacy of divine visitations, as well as underlying principles like faith, fasting, prayer, and holiness in the Wesleyan tradition—all spiritual hallmarks at Asbury.

Pastor's assistance work filled my time for the next two years, first for the Central Methodist Church of Atlantic City. For one church I made eighteen hundred calls in six weeks. The pastor urged me to get the job done so he could send a good report to conference. I was not to take time to pray in the homes. However, this was just after World War I when many hearts were burdened over the loss of sons or fathers, so I often took time to pray. Many dear people were helped and comforted.

The Board of Church Extension gave me the choice of two other jobs. Since these were in a foreign section of the city, I must be very careful about telling folk about Jesus. My heart sank with grief. I resigned and began holding revival meetings.

In the very first meeting, five women came seeking holiness. The pastor was so angry he would not even kneel to pray with them. He said, "These are my best members." But God softened his heart when he saw the joy and victory that came into their lives. He asked me to hold a meeting in his other church. The Lord gave many marked answers to prayer in my evangelistic years (1919-22).

Often in my evangelistic work I met opposition to the truth of holiness, yet the Lord sealed the messages to the satisfaction of many precious souls. In the early days of my ministry, I found opposition hard to understand.

The Bible doctrine of entire sanctification, as taught by John Wesley, has always encountered opposition. When we enjoy the blessing and preach messages that revolve around the fact of a full, free, and present salvation, folks will be fully delivered from sin, its guilt, its power, and its presence within. William Carvosso, the great class leader of England, said, "As holiness is neglected, the work declines; as it is stressed, the work revives."

A dear saint in Bristol, Pennsylvania, asked me to lead a meeting in her home for the promotion of holiness. Many folk found blessing and help. The pastor of this lady's church was opposed to holiness. He reported the meetings to the bishop. I was asked to appear before three preachers and the bishop. When asked to relate about the holiness meetings, I told how the Lord was using the services. The case was dismissed. We went on with the holiness meetings for three years until I felt led to go to Asbury College in Kentucky.

Soon students were asking me to join various organizations. Among others, I joined the Mountain Missionary Society, founded by Claude

Mingledorff in 1915. Its purpose was to take the gospel to the mountains of Eastern Kentucky. Something about this work attracted me. I never missed a meeting.

Before coming to Asbury I had arranged to hold five revivals the next summer. However, a very urgent call came from the Free Methodist Mission in Breathitt County, Ky. They said there was no money in it and that I could face some hard things. I could not get away from this appeal. I cancelled three of the scheduled meetings and started for Eastern Kentucky to spend eight and a half weeks in revivals.

For the first three nights I preached full salvation with much liberty and blessing. The missionaries said, "We feel you are on the wrong track. No one here is ready for holiness. We must get people saved first."

I was new, so I decided to being with preaching on sin and repentance. The meetings began to lose power and conviction. I said, "I must mind God and preach so these dear people will know how God delivers from all sin." I did, and the Holy Ghost honored it. Twenty-three sought the Lord, clear conversions, and over half of these were sanctified later in the revival. This was the first awakening in the history of this community.

While many souls truly prayed through, the devil was powerfully stirred. Some folk openly fought the meeting. I remember one night when they rocked the building. Stones came through the windows; some cracked the weathered boards. Guns were fired, so it was like war outside. My soul was blessed and calm. There was a window back of the pulpit. I thought surely I'll get shot while preaching and go to heaven. God gave me great courage.

Back at Asbury, as chaplain of the Senior Class, I often asked folk to pray for God to call some of the seniors to the mountains of Kentucky. Finally, one of them said, "Miss McConnell, we feel it is almost a joke for you to be making this request. We feel God is calling you."

On my fortieth birthday, June 1, 1924, Dr. Henry Clay Morrison, then President of Asbury College, handed me my diploma and said, "I give this diploma to the General of the Kentucky Mountains."

Along the five thousand creeks and hollows of Eastern Kentucky, more than five hundred thousand Anglo-Saxon people live. In 1924 a Breathitt County lawyer told me, "One fourth of the children between ages seven and thirteen do not attend school. Either their parents do not care, or they do not have money for adequate clothing or books. Their lot is constant toil."

It became known that we wanted to build a boarding school and church in one of the communities. Mr. and Mrs. J. G. Lawson kindly donated twelve acres of land. We set a day to clear the land. Thirty-one people came to help. Snakes ran from their hiding places as small trees, brush, and sumac were cut. The work went very well.

In September Miss Mary Vandiver returned to Asbury. I was left alone in the mountains.

The Lord let my faith be tested to the limit that first hard winter. Not only was I alone and often hungry, but my room was near the ground. Water stood under the house most of the winter. I couldn't keep warm.

Finally, one night I told the Lord, "I'm here until I die, if I starve or if I freeze." That broke the devil's power. I heard him go just like a strong wind. The enemy had tried to defeat me, but God saw I meant business. I have never been tormented like it through the years since.

Soon someone sent me an old canvas piano cover. This was truly a Godsend. Laid between the thin mattress and springs, it helped to keep out the cold. Soon money came. I was able to pay my room rent and get my meals in a restaurant.

For the story of the building of the high school, I have asked R. L. Swauger to write. He tells us,

> In the spring of 1925, just after Asbury commencement, seven young men wended their way to the scene of their labors for the summer, the place later known as "Baby Asbury." It was located on a high hill above the North Fork of the Kentucky River, two miles below the mouth of Frozen Creek.

The young men loved the work and were powerfully blessed as they built, prayed, and sang. In the evenings they held services in the little schoolhouses within three or four miles of the campus. They invariably tell me with deep gratitude how God used that summer to enrich their spiritual lives.

The seven young men were to erect the Administration Building. They established a camp, pitched an army squad tent for living quarters, erected a temporary shed which served as kitchen and dining hall, and laid down a schedule. The order of the day was: rising bell, 4 a.m.; breakfast, 4:30, followed by family prayers and devotions; work at 5:30; dinner at 11:30; supper at 5:30 p.m.

The neighbors across the river tell of hearing songs of praise and voices of prayer. Each boy had a chosen spot in the nearby woods for holding his own "secret" devotions (pp. 28-31).

The building was finished and dedicated September 8, 1925, by Dr. H. C. Morrison and others from Asbury College.

While all the foregoing battles and victories were upon us, we also had many other difficult problems. A twenty-five thousand dollar debt for materials for the first building, and the school running expenses, had to be met. Some of our creditors were getting worried. One was in such distress he threatened to sue us. We held on to God, sometimes fasting for days. I had read *The Life of George Muller*—the great orphanage man of faith of Bristol, England. I felt the Lord wanted us to use a similar plan.

One time the faculty and I fasted and prayed for ten days. God came so near. The entire campus was pervaded with the power of the Holy Ghost. We were praying for eighteen hundred dollars to pay a note. The Lord did exceeding abundantly above. Many times folk in the bank would ask, "How do you do it?" We would tell them the Lord did it all.

Calls began coming for church services in other sections of the mountains. By 1925 we had seventeen preaching points. The influence of the school is felt in every phase of life throughout Eastern Kentucky.

[1]Zachary Taylor Johnson, "The Story of Asbury College," unpublished MSS, 3 vols., 1968, Asbury University Archives; see vol. 2, p. 368.

[2]Delbert Rose, "Other Asbury Happenings," *The Herald*, May 31, 1972, p.11, Asbury University Archives, Asbury Revivals, Box 1, File 1.

[3]Lela McConnell, with Edith Vandewarker, *The Mountain Shall be Thine* (Jackson, KY: Kentucky Mountain Holiness Association, 1989), selected material. Used by permission. All rights reserved.

SNAPSHOTS – Behind the Scenes

Power of Prayer. "It isn't possible to over-estimate the value of prayer. It is efficacious. It has power with God. Earnest faith and prayer, with an eye single to God's glory alone, from a sanctified heart, avails much." Lela McConnell, *The Mountain Shall be Thine.*

Sent Out Two by Two. After graduation, Lela McConnell was accompanied by Mary Vandiver, who agreed to spend the summer before returning for her senior year. A young man by the name of Zachary T. Johnson drove them to the train station. Lela McConnell and Z. T. Johnson would eventually become presidents of Kentucky Bible Institute and Asbury College respectively. Ibid.

First Woman to Receive an Honorary Doctorate. President Z. T. Johnson invited Lela McConnell to the 1947 commencement to receive an honorary doctorate, granted to a person considered to have made an outstanding contribution to human welfare, socially, educationally, and religiously. She was the first woman to receive this award. She received a standing ovation. ATL.

Peace that Surpasses Understanding. Crawford and Glide Halls both burned to the ground in 1924. At the time of the fire President Morrison was returning by train from a speaking engagement in Texas. He had a weakened heart, and students feared that the first sight of this catastrophe would be too much for the old man to bear. The Spirit of God, however, moved upon him as the train passed from

Louisville to Lexington, giving Morrison a sense of peace, come what may. The students were quite surprised to find him so cheerful when he surveyed the damage. ATL.

Farming. In 1915 President Morrison decided to buy a nearby farm property for the college. In his mind a working farm would provide both food for the college dining hall and paid employment for needy students. The farm sold for a profit a few years later, but agriculture played a continuing role in the life of the college. In more recent years, equestrian and sustainable agriculture constitute important new foci. ATL.

The Debt Revival and Financial Freedom. In January, 1909, the college began the year debt-free. The total school property was appraised at forty-five thousand dollars. The debt-free condition did not last. On March 18, a fire began in Music Hall around 6:40 a.m., while everyone was at breakfast. It spread to the Administration Building. A bucket brigade formed, but proved ineffective. The Trustees sold the East Main Street property and shifted college operations to the current North Lexington site. For a short period of time, there was only one bathtub on campus. Asbury faced financial struggles for decades. Near the height of the great depression (1935), students fasted and prayed in what became known as the "debt revival." Within three years the school was debt free and remains so even now. ATL.

Alexander Reid – c1932

INTRODUCTION: Whether in the Appalachian mountains or the heart of Africa, pioneer missionaries helped establish schools, medical facilities, and social-political reforms. They sought to incarnate the gospel of Christ in tangible ways, i.e. "I was hungry and you gave me something to eat... " (Matthew 25:35-40 NIV). But that is not all they did; they also prayed for spiritually dynamic divine-human encounters. Although there is no direct account that he participated in a spontaneous revival as a student, Alexander Reid refers to the influence of Asbury revival. It became his benchmark for how God can change human hearts and social conditions in a way best described as "turbo-charged." As a result, he experienced extraordinary revival in Africa, and in later years prayed for revival in campus prayer meetings.

Reid enrolled at the Asbury College in the immediate wake of the 1921 Asbury awakening. While he was alive, he and his wife inspired Asbury students to enter missionary work, including retired missionary Dr. Phyllis Corbitt, MD, who described to me how thrilled she was to hear reports from "Uncle Alex" when he came to Wilmore on furlough. The following article is adapted from Reid's originals. Parts of it were published by Dr. Thomas Carruth when he was Director of the Prayer Life Movement for the Methodist Church and living in Nashville, Tennessee. (He would later serve as Director of Spiritual Life at Asbury Seminary.) At the time, Carruth said, "This is the greatest prayer report ever received in my office."[1]

In a study of every revival movement across the church we find the prominent place that prayer has taken in every instance.

We went to Africa nearly twenty-eight years ago [NOTE: Reid was writing in late 1957] believing that the Christ who called us to Africa would answer prayer and send us a spiritual awakening in the dark continent, like that we had seen in the halls of Asbury and in the great camp meeting centers of our nation. We called together a group of our missionary friends and proposed we make Friday a day of fasting and prayer until God gave us victory.

Heathen customs of child marriage, polygamy, idol worship, moon worship, fetishes and charms everywhere, wicked funeral rites even to placing people alive with the dead in the grave with the departed humbled our hearts before God and caused us to cry in desperation of soul, "Is there no balm in Gilead? Is there no physician there?" Has not the one who called us here promised us victory if we pray and trust him?

Through more than two years of fasting and prayer and traveling constantly in the villages of our district we held up Christ mighty to save to the uppermost. Then by the hundreds people began reaching out after new life but couldn't grasp the meaning of it. In deep agony of soul we decided to follow the plan Bishop Warne of India had followed in calling our sixty-five preachers and their families together with such as might be interested to study the Book of Acts for ten days and to pray.

The people themselves prepared a palm front tabernacle to protect them from the tropical sun and made the little houses of the same materials. After the two years of fasting and prayer, and about three more days of Bible study and prayer there swept over the multitude something of the same Spirit that prevailed on the day of Pentecost; when the multitude was moved heavenward at one mighty movement which brought thousands of souls to the camp ground to find the same Christ the first praying multitude had found. They scattered the holy fire from village to village, witnessing scenes transcending words to fully describe.

At one district meeting of the preachers following this camp, the preachers reported twenty-two people won to Christ in three months time. This movement spread from village to village for hundreds of miles throughout the whole tribe. Churches sprang up everywhere built by converts to the new faith.... Many witch doctors were gloriously won to Christ and became witnesses of their newfound faith.

For most of the intervening years we have been trying to keep up with this people's movement.... Two years ago it again became necessary to form Lomela district, and now such an evangelistic opportunity is given us that it has been named by the General Conference as one of the "Lands of Decision" for the next quadrennium.... Practically all the present leaders of our Central Conference have been won to Christ through this movement.

From these early fast prayer meetings and the continuation of camp meetings, as part of our evangelistic program in our conference, what rewards are we reaping at the present moment? Allow me to present the statement of Rev. Louis Johnson:

> As the Mbulo la Wedi Umvalambi [the term known and used throughout the tribe to describe the revival and what hap-

pened in the early years—comparable to the early Cane Ridge meetings in Kentucky] and your continuing emphasis on camp meetings and revivals has produced fruit and helped bring a basis for blessings of the Holy Spirit in July 1955... until the church is living in a modern Pentecost.... "Powerful moral and ethical changes are taking place in the lives of these people as they turn from idols and fetishes and charms; adultery, lying, stealing, sins of the flesh and sins of the disposition to Christ. In a quarterly meeting of preachers, a revival visitation campaign was carried on in the most wicked village in the territory, and it was turned upside down in repentance and conversion. The state officials said that Wetshi Mdjadi was the worst place in the territory. They said, "Go win all the people to Christ, we are for you. We have tried everything and nothing else will work." It was truly a people's Christian movement, with the chief and the village elders and several hundred people looking to Jesus for forgiveness and the Christian life.

Following the departure of Mr. Johnson for furlough, the Rev. Mr. Machlin became the District Missionary helper for faithful Moses Ngandjolo, the superintendent, and we quote reports from him.

Nearly all the hundred and forty preachers of the district were there, with representative laymen from their churches.... There were some fifteen hundred present for all the services. As in past revivals, God once again opened the doors of heaven, and poured out blessings such as I, nor most there, had never seen before. Both Superintendent Ngandjolo and pastor Omokoko preached from inspired hearts. Their messages as usual struck at the hearts of those who were present.

Following a brief message, a whole evening was given over to testimony. It lasted for two hours, as people stood to tell how God had saved them from sin. As one man got up, soft whispers rippled across the congregation. Everyone turned to look at him. Roughly, this is what he said: "For the past fifteen years I have had an unquenchable hunger for eating human flesh. I have killed and eaten at least twenty-five people during this period of time. During this revival God has shown me the awfulness of my sin and I have come to Him confessing it and asking Him to give me a new heart. I believe He has done it and has delivered me. I want you to know it and to pray for me." When he sat down, the congregation broke into almost hysterical applause and shouting.

I never witnessed such a spontaneous group movement. Many Christians who had known this man jumped up and began to embrace him, to shake his hands and dance for joy. Other sins confessed covered the complete range of all possible. Restitution was made publicly. If the state officials had been there, they surely would have carted at least half of the crowd away into oblivion on the basis of what they confessed openly.

During 1957and 1958 we had the privilege of giving part-time supervision with Moses Ngandjolo to this district at Lodja.... We were with Dr. Harold Mohn, and he declared that it was a veritable repetition of Pentecost, a rewriting of the Book of Acts. Following his visit to the Congo, he wrote in the February issue of *Methodist Story* the following words:

A great revival is sweeping the Congo. The mass movement in the villages, the fruit of long years of Methodist missionary work, makes vivid our opportunities in this Land of Decision. The doors are not just open—they are off the hinges. The Billy Graham of the Congo is Moses Ngandjolo.... Public confessions at Ngandjolo's services run the gamut of human sin—from moonshining to cannibalism. It is the practice of authorities to make no arrests on the basis of these confessions, and this is the practical reason: the conversion of criminals is a more rapid way to law and order than court action. The people of the Congo are grateful to all who have helped bring them the gospel.... Month after month there have been meetings in other villages with no abatement of interest.[2]

CONCLUSION: Alexander Reid is partly responsible for this anthology. My connection to Dr. Reid began when he launched a weekly noon Friday fast-prayer meeting in 1972. As a new transfer student I occasionally experienced a strong conviction to skip a meal and go to Hughes Auditorium to pray, something which I initially resisted, but to which I belatedly yielded. On one of these occasions I stumbled onto a small group of erstwhile old-timers gathered for prayer, including: J. C. McPheeters, Thomas Carruth, Robert Neff, and Dan Philpot (Rev. Ford Philpot's brother). Dr. Reid began each meeting with comments about the power of fasting and prayer, often punctuating his remarks with accounts of how it birthed explosive people movements to Christ in the heart of Africa. He always inspired Christians to unite with the Friday fast-prayer call, a Wesleyan tradition with Patristic roots.

While attending my forty year Class reunion, I searched for information related to Reid and John Wesley Hughes. In the process I had a discussion about the Asbury revivals with Archival Director Suzanne Gehring. My interest was prompted by a statement made by my former history professor, Dr. Duvon Corbitt, who said rather crustily, "People make a big deal about the revival of 1970; they should have been there for some of the earlier ones!" Suzanne encouraged my interest in a comprehensive overview.

As for Reid, it must be pointed out that European colonial empires began to collapse in the aftermath of the Second World War. The process was often fraught with conflict. This included mission-sponsoring agencies and individual missionaries, some of whom paternalistically assumed that indigenous leaders were not yet ready for "self rule." As a child of his time, Dr. Reid may have been among them in regard to this or other issues of the day. By the 1970s the former Belgian Congo (now the Democratic Republic of Congo) became militantly anti-Christian.[3] Still, Dr. Reid spoke and wrote[4] with awe about saintly African leaders, and through the years he backed his words by sponsoring African students who came to study at Asbury College. In light of all this, Reid's 1972 pamphlet, Our Biblical and Wesleyan Heritage Through Fasting and Prayer,[5] *constitutes a valuable addendum, found at the end of this anthology.*

[1] Alexander J. Reid, "African Story is Called the Greatest to Come to Attention of Director," *Texas Christian Advocate*, Feb. 28, 1958, p. 3, Asbury University Archives, Alexander J. Reid Manuscript Collection, Box 63 Folder 7.

[2] Alexander J. Reid, "Prayer Brings Revival to Africa," *Asbury Alumnus* combined with *Asbury College Bulletin*, April-August in 3 issues, 1959, Asbury University Archives, Alexander J. Reid Manuscript Collection, Box 63 Folder 7.

[3] Alexander J. Reid, *The Roots of Lomomba: Mongo Land* (Hicksville, NY: Exposition Press, 1979), pp. 164-173.

[4] Ibid., p. 192.

[5] Alexander J. Reid, *"Our Biblical and Wesleyan Heritage Through Fasting and Prayer,"* 1972, Asbury University Archives, Alexander J. Reid Manuscript Collection, Box 63 Folder 7.

Student Writers – 1938

INTRODUCTION: The backdrop to the 1938 and the 1942 revivals is the specter of worldwide conflict. Wiser people in 1938 began to think about the prospect of military duty, and by 1942 students were saying goodbye to men and women entering wartime service. Death was more than a blip on their youthful horizons. It grew into a riot down the block, and eventually into armed trespassers in the front yard. The question became personal: "Will our schoolmates who enlisted come home?" For some it also became philosophical: "Assure us the Christian faith is still valid and tell us what we can offer to a world running amuck with the competing claims of fascism, communism, and secularism."

One primary witness, Vice President Z. T. Johnson, concurred that 1938 "makes the cut" as a great revival at Asbury. He wrote, "It has become customary through the years to describe nearly every revival as an outstanding one, sometimes the best in the history of the school. This section, however, will not deal with the ordinary revivals, but only with those that were either spontaneous or which by general observation and consensus of opinion... really were outstanding."[1]

There was a gap of seventeen years following the 1921 revival (not including the important but less spontaneous 1935 depression-era "debt retirement revival"), so something extraordinary was probably unexpected. Thus, the Collegian *announcements contained positive anticipation expressed in a folksy tone, albeit with a call to prayer which would soon be heeded.*

The annual mid-winter revival will begin at the church *[NOTE: Wilmore Methodist Episcopal Church, South]* on Sunday, January 23, 1938. The evangelist for this series of meetings is Dr. Joseph Owen. For a number of years, Dr. Owen was President of John Fletcher College in University Park, Iowa. John Fletcher is a sister school to Asbury College as far as ideals are concerned. It stands for the fundamental doctrines just as Asbury does. When Dr. Owen left John Fletcher as President, the students felt that they had lost a most sympathetic and understanding friend. Young people have always been Dr. Owens' special interest. He has given his life to the helping of the younger generation in their pursuit of life. That does not mean that he has no interest for the older people. He does; but his special interest is the younger folk. It has been said of him that he is forceful and uncompromising, yet tactful and kind in the greatest degree. Mixed into his preaching one can detect a keen sense of humor which makes him liked immediately.

Asburians! Pray for a glorious revival![2]

NOTE: Though this revival came at the end of several regularly scheduled services, it took a surprising and spontaneous turn. The following description is by a student and appeared on the front page of the February 5, 1938, edition of the Collegian.

Great Spiritual Awakening as Asburians Go to Altar

As the mid-winter revival neared a climax, students, citizens, and friends were thrilled by a manifestation which swept the college dining hall Thursday noon. Two hundred seventeen testimonies were heard from the students and faculty. At a hastily arranged altar many found spiritual victory.

A spirit of prayer has hovered round the campus during this special season of revival effort. The spirit of the Lord has been in the prayer services every evening. Dr. Owen has urged each person to be in much prayer.

The message last Monday evening was on prayer. There is no real definition of prayer given in the Bible. If there were, we would all pray that way and no other. But in our praying, our life itself should become a prayer. First, we must pray there is no battle on between prayer and service. Therefore, we can pray constantly. Next, men ought to pray importunately and in faith believing. Expect God to answer our prayers when we pray. Then the thought comes: pray much, talk little, and believe the Lord.

Each one of us has a ministry to do in this life. The masses today do not know God. Something in their lives has caused doubt in a belief of God. We cannot have part of the life spiritual and let the world hang on to the other part of our being. We must be spiritually whole to be at our best for the Master. If we let the Holy Spirit heal the heart, the world can come on and it will not faze us.

We are told that if we ask much, we shall receive much. In our prayer to God, we should ask largely and expect to receive largely. Through prayer we can open up the storehouse of God's blessings....[3]

NOTE: President Z. T. Johnson also recorded his reflections.

The students thought that the definite experience of sanctification and the deeper work of grace were explained so thoroughly by Dr. Owen that it was easy for each one to enter into the experience. The meeting closed with almost universal results among the student body. This revival, unlike the three spontaneous revivals already described, seemed to depend more upon the clarity of the preaching.[4]

NOTE: One week later, the school newspaper contained a short retro-spective piece, calling people to continuing personal transformation and higher goals in life.

...We have just witnessed one of the most victorious revivals in Asbury for some years. The Spirit of Christ has so permeated the campus activities, and hearts of faculty members and students alike, that His praises have been sung by a large majority of our number.

However, if... we settle down into the same rut, forgetting our blessings, we will gradually lose out. If we feel like a deflated balloon instead of a "burning bush" there is something lacking.

The reconstruction of the soul through consecration has been accomplished. The wheels of spiritual peace must be turned by the oil of Prayer.

The great diplomat and statesman, Jesus Christ, is the only power we need. Through Him we live and have our being. By His blood we are cleansed. Because of Him we can be children of God.

It is up to us as Christians to decide whether or not we will succumb to avarice and hate or go forward with Christ.

What will the aftermath of this revival be?

Search your heart, friend. Make Christ your Master and love your weapon. Defeat Satan and temptation with a mighty display of Christ-like living.

Make Christ the aftermath.[5]

CONCLUSION: In addition to testimonies of brokenness leading to victory, we detect themes of sudden surprise, exhilaration, calls to mission, and a sense of God's nearness. As usual, it is difficult to ex-press the sense of God's manifest presence which typically qualifies an episode as an "unusual" revival. Rudolf Otto did a credible job in his exploration of the concept of the "Numinous" or Holy, and his efforts played an important role in the conversion of C.S. Lewis.[6] In 1938 Christ again became Immanuel, God with us.

Unfortunately, more personal details were unavailable. There appear to be no clear-cut accounts by living witnesses from the 1938 Revival. (They would be graduates age 95 or above.) But I had delightful sessions with a few of Asbury's oldest surviving alums. Also, I was fortunate to have had visits with Dr. Dennis Kinlaw, who helped to round out the picture of another episode, the 1942 revival.

[1] "Dr. Joseph Owen to Open Mid-Winter Revival on Sunday," *Collegian Collection*, Vol. 23 No. 13, Saturday, January 22, 1938, page 1, Kinlaw Library Archives and Special Collections, Asbury University. Adapted.

[2] Johnson, "The Story of Asbury College," Vol. 2, p. 350.

[3]*Great Spiritual Awakening as Asburians Go to Altar*, Collegian Collection, Vol. 23, No. 13, Saturday Feb. 5, 1938, p. 1.

[4]Johnson, "The Story of Asbury College," Vol. 2, p. 371.

[5]Buddie Cole, "Aftermath," *Collegian Collection*, Vol. 23, No. 15, Saturday, Feb. 12, 1938, p. 2.

[6]Clara Sorrocco, "Surprised by Awe: C.S. Lewis & Rudolf Otto's Idea of the Holy," *Touchstone Magazine*, July/August 2011.

Nancy Crary Ridley – 1938

INTRODUCTION: Nancy Crary was a faithful diarist throughout her college years (1937-1941). She was a freshman living in Glide-Crawford dormitory during the 1938 revival, at times confined to a wheelchair after an accident and a foot infection. She missed chapel when the spiritual "fire" first began to fall in late January. As the week unfolds, her writing displays excited tones as numerous students experienced significant encounters with God.

January 29 – God's spirit <u>surely</u> is working here. Grayson was saved and Vangie was sanctified in chapel....

January 30 – When they got home from church, Corrie had such a burden that she, Dee, Vangie, and Ginnie went to Vangie's room and prayed until one a.m. Wonderful blessing!

February 1 – I missed another wonderful chapel service and also testimonies in the dining hall, but won't miss any more.

February 2 – There were testimonies in the dining hall after breakfast, then again at noon.

February 3 – What a wonderful day of God's presence this has been! With others, Joe really was saved, shouting and crying. At the dining hall, testimonies (230 of them) lasted two hours.

[NOTE: Over a period of nine days, Nancy mentions the names of students who connected with Christ—Corrie, Dee, Becky, Grayson, Vangie, Martha Joe, Wright, Tex, Gillie, Paul, Emory, Hatchell, "Pud," Jean, and Butch. Her boyfriend at that time, Butch, understandably received a little more attention than most.]

Butch came down to the conservatory in the morning, then after supper we talked, and when Dr. Owen gave the altar call that evening, he and Tex went up but didn't settle anything. He came back to tell me he would pray through in his room. Martha and I went home and prayed.

February 4 – Dottie came back with Nell and talked with me about Butch. It's not faith with him. Morrison Hall had a prayer meeting and then they prayed in Bill's room until 12:30 a.m.

February 5 – Dr Owen gave a good talk on victorious living in chapel. Butch and I talked about being saved. In the evening Dr. Owen preached on "if we neglect." Pud went to the altar; when he got through, his mother shouted. A group prayed with Butch and then he left and prayed with Dr. Moore and was saved.

February 6 – As we came out of the dining hall after breakfast, Butch and Gillie were on the roof of Fletcher Dormitory, flying like kites.

Z. T. Johnson, Dennis and Elsie Blake Kinlaw – 1942

INTRODUCTION: This narrative is a compilation of various sources woven into one, principally a personal interview with Dr. Dennis Kinlaw, written memoirs by Dr. Z. T. Johnson and a 1942 Collegian article, written by Dennis Kinlaw. As happened several other years, the revival of 1942 took a spontaneous and extraordinary turn.

Elsie Blake's Sunday School teacher at the Methodist Church in Schenectady, New York, was the spouse of an interim pastor. She told her high school girls that going to church was not enough; they needed to accept Christ personally. This was a somewhat unusual idea in Elsie's congregation. Nevertheless, that night Elsie knelt down by her bed and opened the door of her heart to the Savior. Later the teacher instructed the girls to ask God about which college to attend.

By some odd coincidence, shortly thereafter Elsie's father saw the interim pastor himself and the subject of colleges arose. The pastor said, "I'm not sure I'd send my children to a good many of these East Coast colleges." He'd seen bad results, with young people straying from the faith. Elsie's father asked for a recommendation. The pastor said, "Asbury College near Lexington, Kentucky." Mr. Blake went home to announce to Elsie that she needed to look at Asbury. But sitting on the kitchen table was a catalogue—from Asbury College. Mr. Blake inquired, "Where did that come from?" Elsie replied, "I read about Asbury in an almanac and sent for their catalogue." Asbury was a pretty name that matched her mental picture of horses and Kentucky Bluegrass. God was at work ahead of Elsie's father.

At Asbury, Dennis Kinlaw heard Elsie Blake give her testimony at a student event. The next day he started chasing her. He says that he chased her for sixty-four years. On one occasion she went to the altar. In those days some Christians still spoke about experiences like the inner witness of the Holy Spirit and entire sanctification. What transpired we do not entirely know, but she did tell Dennis, "I did not go back to my room alone last night." With an initial and second working of God's grace in her bloodstream, Elsie found herself led to the center of campus spiritual life.

Along with others, she helped organize prayer chains and prepare altar workers for a planned 1942 autumn revival.

NOTE: The "planned revival" took a powerful, spontaneous turn, as reported by President Z. T. Johnson.

The revival of 1942 was held in September as the fall revival for the college. It was led by Rev. Dwight Ferguson of Cardington, Ohio. Special prayer meetings were held all over the campus, and special groups were organized for personal work, with a committee working in each dormitory, attempting to get every student to attend each service, and to assist every student who needed spiritual help.

One morning there was a great chapel service in which dozens of students came to the altar and prayed through. The service lasted most of the morning. At the noon meal that day, students began to testify, and the presence of the Holy Spirit was recognized in a most unusual way. After the meal, the students gathered in front of the Administration Building in great numbers, and began to testify from the porch and steps. Great rejoicing followed and many hands were lifted in prayer.[1]

NOTE: In the afterglow of this spiritual outpouring, Dennis Kinlaw, then a student religion editor with the Asbury Collegian, wrote of it:

A GOOD BEGINNING

As this week closes on our campus, our hearts are filled with unusual joy in the Lord because of the way God has worked in our midst. God has done the exceeding abundant above all that we dared ask or think, and we have had a week of unusual victory. Truly our hearts should be overflowing with a praise something like that which flooded the soul of David when he wrote "Bless the Lord, O my soul and all that is within me, Bless His holy name. " We have good reason to rejoice in Him today.

As we look back over the last few days, we are reminded of another unusual manifestation of God's power, one that took place about two millenniums ago at Pentecost. The same God that descended upon the disciples there in the upper room is the God that has come upon us and been in our midst these days.

As we think of this, there is one thought that comes from Pentecost that would be profitable for us to remember. Pentecost was not just a time of great blessing and joy for the disciples. It was also a time of equipping—equipping for days of toil and battle that were ahead. It was the divine means of preparing God's workmen.

As the revival closes, it is easy for us to let down spiritually. The tendency is to say that since we are saved and sanctified, everything is all right with us. We make crisis experiences an end in themselves. However, God never intended that it should be that way. Pentecost was a means to an end, preparation as a means to service later. So with an experience of conversion or sanctification. We must not stop there. That is but God's preparation for us to live a life of service to Him.

A crisis experience such as we get at sanctification is much like a door; but of what use is a door without a house? It is but the avenue in. Let us not stop now with just an experience, but rather let us press on in our new-found victories into the land of promise that God has for us, a holy life. Things are not over now. They have just begun.[2]

NOTE: Skip forward twenty-eight years. In the wake of the 1970 revival, then college President Dr. Dennis Kinlaw articulated a similar perspective. Looking back he wrote,

Two questions have been common in the last six weeks as those of us at Asbury have talked with others. The first was, "When will it end?" When it became obvious that the presence of the Spirit on the campus was continuing, the question became, "How long will it last?" God's works are not acts of passing fancy but movements with long-range designs. The most exciting part of this period of blessing is yet to come.... More clearly than ever people have heard God's voice saying, "Whom shall I send and who will go for me?" Their faces are now lifted to the future and to the problems that confront our world. Revival time is a time of gathering of workers. In the past, revival times have prepared the Church for persecution or for service. The purpose of the present movement may be for both. Let us pray that it will at least accomplish the latter.[3]

CONCLUSION: How about the present? Only God knows what lies ahead. Now is the time for young disciples to prepare. God will enable them to become more than adequate for the challenges and opportunities that lie ahead.

[1]Johnson, *The Story of Asbury College*, Vol. 2., p. 171-172.

[2]Dennis Kinlaw, *The Asbury Collegian*, October, 1942, page 2.

[3]Dennis Kinlaw, "To God be the Glory," *Ambassador Magazine*, April, 1970, p.3.

SNAPSHOTS – Challenging Times

No Salary for the President. Perhaps because he appealed to *The Herald* readers so regularly for money for Asbury, in September, 1917, H. C. Morrison explained to them how little he profited personally from his connection to the college. He declared that he had received no salary during the seven years since becoming President, and in fact he often donated part of his private camp meeting earnings to the college as well. ATL.

The Difference Dreamers Make. Mrs. Elizabeth Glide was a wealthy convert living in San Francisco. A keen admirer of President and Mrs. Morrison, she donated $50,000 for a new women's dormitory in 1920, and another $20,000 for a seminary building, Morrison Hall, in 1922. Mrs. Glide and her pastor, J. C. McPheeters, dreamed of starting a West Coast version of Asbury Seminary in association with her home church, Glide Memorial Methodist, in San Francisco. The effort never came to fruition, partly due to Dr. McPheeters' shift to the presidency of Asbury Theological Seminary after the death of H. C. Morrison in 1943. By this time the seminary was situated across the street from the college. It had one all-purpose building, five faculty, sixty students, a $15,000 budget, no endowment, precarious accreditation, and no assured income. The search committee indicated that without Dr. McPheeters the school would probably have to close. The situation looked hopeless, but he came anyway. Consider the seminary now. *Pardon Me, Sir... Your Halo's Showing: The Story of J. C. McPheeters*

Kissing Away the Challenges in World War Two. Many students went to war from 1943 to 1945. The campus ratio of men to women was 154 to 429 in September 1944. Phyllis Corbitt, MD, tells how those who remained—rich and poor—all pitched in to help harvest the campus corn crop. One tradition sweetened the work. If a boy or girl found a red ear of corn, they got to kiss the person of their choosing (purportedly a little peck on the cheek). Apparently, even wartime had its advantages.

Robert Barefoot – 1950

INTRODUCTION: But for their tragic deaths shortly after the 1950 Revival, Bob Barefoot and Herbert Van Vorce might be writing their own story. I write "story" rather than "stories" because of the way God intertwined these two very dissimilar individuals to ignite the campus with heavenly glory. The primary source is Halls Aflame, *by Henry C. James and Paul Rader, supplemented by a few reminiscences from others.*

Bob Barefoot didn't have enough money to attend Asbury College. He was a poor Native American from North Carolina who believed God wanted him to attend Asbury. President Z. T. Johnson obviously concurred, listening to this unusual young man and arranging financial assistance through campus work and other financial assistance.[1] People described Bob in various ways, including "a large bear" and "idiosyncratic." A smiling and happy young man, for him no one was a stranger; he characteristically hugged people after being introduced. Beneath it all lay one overriding attribute, a passionate love for the Lord, which resulted from personal tragedy.

He had been severely tested and tried as a student, and because of sickness and a particular physical condition almost lost his faith. Because of this, he spent much time in prayer. He became especially interested in three of his fellow students and prayed earnestly for their conversion. He said later that he had prayed for weeks to God for these men and for a revival which would sweep the campus.[2]

One of these students was a 6'4" senior, Herbert Van Vorce. Herbie and Bob were very different.

> When Herbert Van Vorce came to Asbury College he brought with him an impressive record as an athlete in high school, having been offered a scholarship to one of the leading colleges of this country. Tall, well built, he was handsome and personable. It wasn't long before he was as popular as any other boy on campus. But in spite of the fact that his father, Major H. J. Van Vorce, Army Chaplain and a man of God, gave him a strong Christian background, "Herbie" was skeptical of Christian truth. Before long his name headed many a godly student's list of most wanted men for Christ."[3]

Circumstances came to a head in February 1950. A number of spiritual awakenings were going on across the country, including a powerful spiritual student movement arising in Forest Park, California, Billy Graham's Los Angeles Crusade, and a move of God's Spirit at Wheaton College in January (there was a one-page write-up about it in *Time* magazine), to name a few. How much students at Asbury knew about all this is hard to tell. Regardless, it was God's time for Asbury and an outpouring that would become well-known in the media. The story was second only to a national coal strike.

> The night before the revival started, Herbie was trying to study in his room at Morrison Cottage, but conviction became so great that study was impossible. He left his work, went downstairs, and awakened a fellow student whom he asked to pray with him. The two boys went to a car and had a season of prayer, but Herbie could not seem to pray through. He suggested getting Bob Barefoot, whom he knew had been praying for months that he would make a full surrender to Christ. As they neared the dorm, they met Bob and he told them he was coming to hunt Herbie, because God had told him Herbie needed help.[4]

They went to an empty gym and began crying out to the Lord. One observer who happened to be passing by late at night was Robert

"Clem" Coleman. He found it strange that people were making such a racket in a darkened gym. About three in the morning the fire fell. Van Vorce would later tell people that the power of God came on him so strongly that he lay on the floor for a very long time as though dead.

The morning chapel service took an unusual turn, to say the least. After special guests Rev. and Mrs. Dee Cobb sang, Rev. Cobb prepared to preach. "A holy hush settled down as he was to begin the message. At that moment Robert Barefoot stood for a word of praise for a prayer meeting which a group of boys had the night before where a number of them had found the Lord."[5] Herb Van Vorce jumped to his feet and said he was one of them and that he had been about to go out of Asbury without God. Others followed. Rev. Cobb recalled:

> It was as though an electric shock moved over the whole place, and there was such a sense of the presence of God that one felt almost as though he could reach out and touch Him. From where I stood I would probably best describe it as something like a gentle breeze sweeping across a broad field of wheat. Everyone seemed moved, tears started down some cheeks, and a rapture of delight stirred some to gentle laughter. All over the auditorium young people were standing. Then some, weeping, started to the altar. From then on it was like feasting on the heavenlies.[6]

Dr. W. W. Holland was Chairman of the Department of Philosophy and Religion at the time. He wrote,

> So mighty was the presence of the Holy Spirit in that chapel service that the students could not refrain from testimony. The guest speaker had little opportunity for his message. The floodgates of heaven lifted and God moved into our midst as I have never before witnessed. The Holy Spirit fell upon the entire audience and everything broke loose. Testimonies were followed by confessions, confessions by crowded altars, crowded altars gave place to glorious spiritual victories, and this in turn to more testimonies. Thus it ran for several days,

wave after wave of glory swept the vast audiences; triumph after triumph took place at the altar. At times the Divine Presence was so pronounced that one could gather some conception of what Paul must have experienced when he was caught up into the Third Heaven.[7]

The 1950 "mega" revival was underway.

CONCLUSION: Bob Barefoot did not live very long. After graduation he returned to North Carolina to engage in ministry. He was killed by a drunk driver while offering to assist at the site of an accident. His wife was at his bedside while he was dying; all he could talk about was how beautiful heaven looked.

[1]"Isaac Patton," *Memories of the Asbury Revival of 1950*, Marion Walker, Editor. Unpublished Manuscript, 2000, AUA, pp. 26, 31.

[2]Joseph A. Thacker, *Asbury College: Vision and Miracle* (Nappanee, IN: Evangel Press, 1990), p. 199.

[3]Henry C. James and Paul Rader, *Halls Aflame*, pp. 34-35.

[4]Ibid., p. 35.

[5]Ibid., p. 8.

[6]Joseph A. Thacker, *Asbury College: Vision and Miracle,* p. 198.

[7]Henry C. James and Paul Rader, *Halls Aflame*, p. 9.

Herbert Van Vorce – 1950

INTRODUCTION: The previous story recounts the conversion of Herbert Van Vorce to Christ and the beginning of the 1950 revival. The following portion consists primarily of letters he wrote to his parents and a selection by a newspaper reporter.[1] Refer to the book Halls Aflame to place this material in context.

Immediately, Herbie began to witness to his new-found faith. Every- where he found opportunities to challenge others with what Christ could do in their lives. Herbie wrote his parents soon after he was converted and told of what God was doing.

It is Sunday again; I can truly say it has been one of the best Sundays of my life. Dwight Mikkelson and I with a few others went to Nicholasville to the jail and had a service and then went to Lexington and had a street meeting. We saw a man about fifty years of age gloriously saved. We went down in the slums for the service. However, the man that was saved was a middle class man whom we met uptown and had given a tract.... After talking a while, he said he would like to become a Christian. We went over to the car and the man was gloriously saved.

Without doubt you have already sensed a change in my life. The other morning at three o'clock in the gym I settled it all with God. I started praying at twelve and at about three o'clock the fire fell. I put everything on the altar: Lois, my life ambition, everything. I don't know, but God has been revealing sermon after sermon to me. It wouldn't surprise me if He had the ministry in mind for me. I am going ahead and will continue trying to get into medical school, trusting that God's will shall be worked out. I can say I never had such a glorious revelation of the Holy Spirit as I had the other night. God has been so gracious to me by giving me Christian parents who will take their stand for Jesus Christ and the fullness of His Spirit.

I haven't had a good night's sleep for two weeks until last night. Every night there would be a text running through my mind. I don't feel like a radical or that I am emotionally upset. I know what I want and settled it with God for time and eternity.

Well, folks, I love you and I felt I should let you know about my change and complete submission to God. Pray for me; I know you do without my asking.

The next letter was written about two or three days later:

How I wish you were here; it is wonderful what the Lord is doing. I have such peace and joy I can't express it. I can't write much because I have been in Heaven for three days, eaten three meals, had about three blessings and walked about three hundred miles telling people that Jesus saves. I have asked I don't know how many merchants in town to come and get right with God. It is an outpouring of the Spirit. People are coming from all over, trying to figure it out and can't conceive of people shouting, getting to God. I am glad I didn't wait for this to make my decision for Christ. I have victory like I never had before. God has laid His hand on me. I am burning up for Jesus; Praise His Name! Dad, I have got what you got; I have it to stay. I am intoxicated with the Spirit; I can hardly write; my body feels like it is floating in heaven. I have caught hold of the hem of His garment. I am on the gospel train that will stop at Hallelujah station. I know you think I am going crazy but God has so wonderfully got hold of me.

Reporters have been here from all over; you probably have heard about it. The revival is now headed for the seventieth hour without stopping.

NOTE: By the time this third letter was written, Herbert and a team of students had returned to Wilmore after holding meetings in Mississippi.

God has marvelously helped me with my work; I am all caught up ready to start studying for finals next week. If it is God's will, I am going back to Mississippi. Dr. Anderson spoke in the capitol building. No definite reports yet on that service.

The Lord has so wonderfully blessed me I could never write in ink or explain in words what has been happening. I am going to the Church of the Open Door Sunday in Louisville, KY. Pray much for this service. Then I have an invitation to go to North Carolina in the First Methodist Church in Durham for a week's meeting and a week-end meeting in Fort Valley, Georgia. Oh, I am anxious to see souls saved.

The revival in Mississippi is spreading throughout the state; we are getting calls from fifteen or twenty towns wanting someone to come for city-wide meetings. Oh, the power of God and how he can use us when we completely forget self and plunge in with God.

It all seems like a dream; I have been singing and testifying in huge churches and over radio stations that cover nine states—potentially thirty million people. It is unbelievable what God has done for me.

Herbie was the first victory of the revival, a babe in Christ, yet his witness had an immediate effectiveness that many a mature minister could not claim. For the next year and a half Herbie continued to grow in grace. God used him mightily in bringing young people to Christ.

Herbie was killed instantly by an electric shock on August 25, 1951, while engaged in construction work. One of the last messages to his family was: "If you ever get a telegram saying I have gone unexpectedly, don't worry, I will be WITH JESUS!" It is estimated that several hundred persons found Christ during a brief year and a half as a result of Herbie's testimony....

CONCLUSION: *Like Bob Barefoot, Herbie Van Vorce died soon after the revival. The following recounts Mr. Van Vorce's reactions to his son's untimely death.*

At the funeral service, in Wilmore, Herbie's father, Chaplain H. J. Van Vorce, asked to give his son's testimony.... Herbie had phoned his folks in Texas:

Dad, I have good news for you and Mom. At three o'clock this morning in the old gym I said: "Lord, you can have my life, my all, for the ministry or the mission field or whatever you want." A week later he phoned again: "Dad, you must come to Wilmore! The greatest revival I have ever seen is here. I did not know it could be so wonderful. We have left this world and have gone to another.

As he stood beside the casket where lay the body of his son, Chaplain Van Vorce closed his remarks by saying:

I do not question the love of God. I am going back to camp with new determination to preach the love of God and His power to sustain through the darkest hours! ...God's will is our will. My hope and prayer is that the mantle of his life might fall on some other boy or boys that they may go forth to do even greater things that Herbie could have done.

[1]Henry C. James and Paul Rader, *Halls Aflame*, pp. 35-38.

Clifford and Sue Mayo – 1950

INTRODUCTION: The following account by Clifford and Sue Mayo is self-explanatory. The source is Marion Walker's unpublished collection. It underscores the historical and spiritual connections between Asbury College and Asbury Theological Seminary.

Clifford had been used to having an early prayer meeting at Cone, Texas, where we pastored before coming to Wilmore. There Clifford enrolled in seminary and I enrolled in Asbury College in January of 1950. Clifford told Elton (E. A.) Mills about wanting to continue early morning prayer meeting at the seminary and Elton said he'd join him.

They began daily prayer meetings in early January, 1950, our first quarter there. They met together in the prayer room at the seminary from 5:00 - 6:00 a.m., as I remember. They prayed for revival to come to both Asbury campuses. Occasionally they were joined by Vincent Rutherford. They read Scripture, prayed for revival, and for each other's prayer requests. They then sang a song as they closed their sessions.

Early in their prayer session on the morning that revival broke out at the college in chapel service, Clifford received a witness, and exclaimed, "It's coming!" Elton asked, "What?" Clifford said, "Revival, don't you know?" Later that morning, I (Sue) was in attendance in the chapel service when the presence of the Holy Spirit invaded and revival was on! I was sanctified that morning! Those were precious days for us!

[1] "Clifford and Sue Mayo," *Memories of the Asbury Revival of 1950*, M. Walker, ed., p. 52.

WHAT IS "*PRAYING THROUGH*"?

From time to time we read that someone "prayed through." The saying surfaces multiple times in these pages. "Prevailing prayer" is a related expression. What does it mean to pray through?

Someone senses an unusual burden to pray for a person or situation, and then they intercede for God's help until the burden is lifted, usually with an assurance that the answer has come. Quite simply, it means praying until we feel assured the request will be fulfilled.

For example, Sheila had a burden to pray one night. Not knowing the situation or even quite what she was sensing, she prayed for two hours. The burden lifted and she had a sense of peace that the answer had come. She found out later that the person she prayed for was in a car wreck at the time she was praying. Almost miraculously no one was hurt!

Praying through draws on scriptural sources. On the eve of his death, Jesus told the apostle Peter, "Simon, Simon, behold, Satan demanded to have you, that he might sift you like wheat, but I have prayed for you that your faith may not fail. And when you have turned again, strengthen your brothers" (Luke 22:31-32, ESV). James writes, "The effective, fervent prayer of a righteous man avails much" (James 5:16, NKJV). Hannah's request for a child in travailing prayer illustrates praying through (1 Samuel 1).

Does God always answer our prayers? Yes, but not always as we think. Jesus prayed that the cup of Calvary be removed; it was not. Prayer does not erase mystery, but neither does mystery erase prevailing prayer. Someone wisely said, "The real tragedy is not unanswered prayer, but unoffered prayer." Sometimes God sends a burden to pray until the answer comes. No one knows until they try.

Old-timers knew something about praying through and travailing prayer. The old paths may be less traveled, but they are still worth using. The testimonies of Clifford Mayo, Robert Barefoot, and Jeannine Brabon illustrate some occurrences at Asbury.

Robert Coleman – 1950

INTRODUCTION: Robert Coleman's story intersects with at least two of the central figures in the 1950 revival, Bob Barefoot and Herbert Van Vorce. Robert was a seminary student serving three small congregations in southern Indiana in his "spare time." His soon-to-be wife, Marietta, was enrolled at Asbury College.

Late one night Robert Coleman, affectionately known as "Clem" to his friends, was walking outdoors when he heard some loud noises emanating in the distance from the college gymnasium. A midnight athletic event... in the dark? Strange indeed. Clem simply continued on his way.

Inside the gym Bob Barefoot—a large, loving and spiritually on-fire college senior—and several other students were praying with Herbert Van Vorce, a notable campus hold-out in regard to Christ.

The next day Marietta, Coleman's fiancée, excitedly told him about an unusual revival taking place in Hughes Auditorium. After visiting the scene, he returned to his studies and then retired to his accommodations at Asbury Theological Seminary, directly across the street from its sister institution, Asbury College. He awoke at three to four in the morning, and noticed the lights still on at Hughes. His curiosity piqued, he decided to investigate. Since it was cold with traces of snow upon the ground, he donned an overcoat over his pajamas and walked down the hall, rousing a few other seminary students on his way. Did anyone want to join him? He had one sleepy-eyed taker.

Approaching the main outer doors on Hughes's east side, Clem felt an almost magnetic pull toward the front of the auditorium. Throwing all caution to the wind, he literally ran to the altar and fell upon his knees, where other students knelt in prayer. He overheard someone say, "Look, it's the preacher Clem Coleman." A student asked, "Clem, will you pray for us?" As he prayed with them, one discerning student sensed that Clem *himself* (as he humbly relates) needed prayer. Dr. Coleman recalls that he was praying in the old King James English style. Elegant as it may be, it seemed somehow amiss in that situation. One small digression is in order.

It's helpful to recall the dominant style of public prayer at that time in Protestant circles. One of Asbury's most notable graduates is Rosalind Rinker (incidentally, still a student during the 1942 campus revival). Here is a short introduction to Rosalind herself, followed by the light she shed on the issue of prayer.

> Born April 2, 1906, converted at the age of fifteen, Rinker sailed to China at the age of twenty to work for OMS, Oriental Mission Society International (later, One Mission Society). She served in China for fourteen years as a secretary, teacher, and evangelist.
>
> As the political climate in China became dangerous, Rinker came back to the U.S. and enrolled at Asbury College in Wilmore, Kentucky. Upon graduating in 1945, she began working as a counselor for InterVarsity Christian Fellowship.
>
> Rinker wrote extensively, which resulted in many speaking engagements. Many of these engagements were workshops based on her well-known book, *Prayer: Conversing with God* [1959], which taught Christians about the art of conversational prayer.
>
> In October 2006, *Christianity Today Magazine* published its list of "The Top 50 Books That Have Shaped Evangelicals" (over the past 50 years). Rinker's *Prayer: Conversing with God* was voted number one on that list by *CT*'s editors. The magazine had this to say: "In the 1950s, evangelical prayer was characterized by Elizabethan 'wouldsts' and 'shouldsts.' Prayer meetings were often little more than a series of formal prayer speeches. Then Rosalind Rinker taught us something

revolutionary: Prayer is a conversation with God. The idea took hold, sometimes too much (e.g., 'Lord, we just really wanna...'). But today evangelicals assume that casual, collo-quial, intimate prayer is most authentic."[1]

Clem stopping praying out loud. Some students gathered around him and began to intercede. God was drawing one of His sons, Robert E. Coleman, to an invisible heavenly altar (Hebrews 4:26, 10:22). Near dawn he experienced a deeper work of God's grace. Something new happened. It was one of the important spiritual junctures in his life. His life and ministry would never be the same.

CONCLUSION: Dr. Robert E. Coleman married his beloved Marietta and acquired academic degrees at Asbury, Princeton, and the University of Iowa. In 1955 he began a lengthy tenure as the first professor of Evangelism at Asbury Theological Seminary. While there he developed a close friendship with Billy Graham, to whom he was introduced in 1956 by a Navigator staff member (that is, his younger brother, Lyman Coleman, of later Serendipity Bible *fame). Robert taught at Asbury Theological Seminary for twenty-seven years, then went to Trinity Evangelical Divinity School for eighteen years. While at Trinity he also led the Institute of Evangelism in the Billy Graham Center at Wheaton College and served as Dean of the Billy Graham International Schools of Evangelism overseas. In 2001 he went to Gordon-Conwell Seminary, near Boston, as the Distinguished Senior Professor of Discipleship and Evangelism. He is the author of twenty-eight books, including the classic* The Master Plan of Evangelism, *published in 1962, with cumulative sales approaching four million copies. Outside the classroom, he was a founding member of the Lausanne Committee on World Evangelization and has ministered in countless churches, colleges, universities, student gatherings, evangelistic crusades, retreats, revival meetings, Keswick conventions, and pastors' conferences around the world.*

[1]Digital location, asbury.edu/offices/library/archives/biographies/rosalind-rinker

Henry James – 1950, 1958, 1970

INTRODUCTION: Reverend Henry James, nicknamed "Penny," witnessed three Asbury revivals. A native of Wilmore, he lives there in retirement with his wife Dorothy.

As a colorful side note, Penny James was not particularly fond of the male students at Asbury College. He was a teenager when World War II burst upon the world. Still too young to enlist, Penny and his high school buddies figured the college boys were draft dodgers. Matters came to a head when they tried to pick a fight. Unknown to them, the college group included a military veteran trained in ju-jitsu. The veteran issued a challenge. "Choose your best guy; the two of us will fight and settle things." Their best man was a giant with a reputation for fighting. They went at it. Penny and his friends never bothered the college boys again.

In February 1950 Penny sensed something unusual on campus. A nominal believer at best, Penny nevertheless decided to check out what would become a life-changing encounter with God.

In 1949 I finished high school and began work at the Wilmore Post Office as a substitute mail carrier; I carried special deliveries on a Whizzer motor bike. Then on February 23, 1950, a great spontaneous revival swept the Asbury College campus. Since we delivered the *Louisville Courier Journal* and other papers at the post office, I began to read about the revival and marveled at the pictures taken by news reporters. For some reason I became very interested in what was taking place.

Out of curiosity one Saturday night I decided to go to the campus to see for myself. This was the day of the week that you might find me at the movies in Nicholasville. (Yes, there was a theater there at that time where we paid ten cents to get in.) At other times I might go down across the railroad tracks to a friend's house where several of us would gather to gamble by playing cards or rolling dice. Incidentally, I found that gambling can be addictive.

From my earliest childhood I had been on the college campus countless times to deliver mail or to go to the gymnasium to watch basketball games. This night was different from all the other times I had walked across the campus.

As I set foot on the ground at the exit end of the semi-circle about 9:30 p.m., I immediately sensed that I was experiencing something that I had never felt before, something I could not explain. It was as if I was intruding on sacred soil and I was reluctant to continue, but I continued toward Hughes Auditorium. At that time I had very little knowledge of the Bible and rarely attended church.

I was alone and it was very quiet except for the singing in the auditorium, so I entered the door on the right ground floor and walked up to the balcony. I hesitated momentarily before entering the service, and a feeling swept over me that is difficult to explain. No one was near me. A strong pulling sensation swept over my body. The best way I can explain it is that it felt as though someone had placed a huge magnet down at the altar and I was being pulled toward it like a piece of iron.

Then and there, I knew this movement of God was not man-made, but supernatural. Later, as I began to study the Scriptures, the answer came in John 12:32, "And I, if I be lifted up from the earth, will draw all men unto me."

I entered the balcony and settled in the middle of the first row of seats. For some time I listened to the testimonies, prayers, and singing of the great hymns. The testimonies were so sincere and honest that one could sense the presence of God in a mighty way. As I listened the burden of my sins became extremely heavy as students told what God was doing in their lives. They boldly related how they had not lived up to the way the Lord wanted them to live and confessed to various sins. There was such an overwhelming presence of God that I felt I could almost reach out and touch Him.

I lingered as long as I could, then the thought hit me, if I failed to respond at this time, I might never have another opportunity like this again. Under deep conviction, with a heavy burden of sin and guilt, I began to make my way to the altar, which seemed so incredibly far away.

There I poured out my heart to God in prayer and repentance. It was about 1:30 a.m., when God removed the burden, which seemed like a ton. I shouted for joy because my chains fell off and I was free from the burden of sins that had bound me for so long. No wonder John 8:36 became my favorite Bible verse: "If the son therefore shall make you free, ye shall be free indeed."

That night I entered Hughes Auditorium with a heart full of hatred for my mother and others and a dislike for Asbury College and Asbury Theological Seminary, but when I left the building the next morning I was a new creature. I had the joy and peace I had sought so long. The things I once hated I now loved and the things I used to love lost their attraction for me. Left on the altar were my heavy burden of sin and a huge puddle of tears. I received a heart transplant that night. God took my heart of stone and gave me a soft heart of love for others and for him.

The next day the sun shone brighter and life seemed wonderful, since I was freed from sin and alive to God. However, little did I know that my spiritual battles had just begun and that they would follow me to this very day.

I was most fortunate to have been present during two other revivals at Asbury College. Converted in the 1950 movement, I was working at the seminary when the 1958 and 1970 revivals came to the campus. I have never ceased to be amazed at the creativity of the Holy Spirit during these great movements of God.

Each one was spontaneous and yet different in various ways. Each came in the month of February, and all were started by praying students. There were no announcements of special speakers or singers, yet as soon as word spread that revival had broken out, people from the city and state immediately joined the services.

The story of the 1970 revival is recorded in *One Divine Moment*, which includes a chapter I contributed entitled, "Campus Demonstrations." The 1950 revival is recorded in *God's People Revived*, which I wrote in 1957. Dr. Paul Rader, former President of Asbury College and a student at Asbury Seminary during the 1958 Revival, co-authored the book *Halls Aflame,* which includes an expansion of *God's People Revived* and a sequel about the 1958 Revival.

In conclusion, people would travel great distances just to be present during these marvelous meetings. If one should ask me to explain in one word the secret of these great movements, I would have to say obedience. Obedience is the pathway to prayer.

CONCLUSION: On April 7, 2015, Penny turned eighty-six. He treasures those divine moments when God opened the heavens and came down. He would be happy to see it happen again.

Robert Wiley – 1950

INTRODUCTION: This is the first of three shorter stories. They remind us not to overlook how campus religious awakenings affected family members of faculty and students caught up in the excitement.

For example, children are affected. Bob Wiley was still in grade school when his father (a professor), and his mother (a gifted vocalist) experienced deepened relationships with God. Several years later Bob was a sophomore at Asbury during the 1958 revival, but he is quick to point out that the revival of 1950 changed his life more. Today he is a retired surgeon, a keen supporter of missionary work, and a long-term member of the Asbury University Board of Trustees. This is his personal account.

In the winter of 1950, when I was ten years old, I vividly remember how the Lord sent a revival to Asbury College. I recall being in Hughes Auditorium and observing students and adults kneeling and praying at the altar, then rising to their feet and lining up on the platform to give testimony how God had convicted them of sin and transformed their lives. As a boy I could sense the presence and the power of the Holy Spirit in the lives of those present.

My father, Professor R. F. Wiley, Sr., participated with other faculty members in the leadership, monitoring the activities and conduct of the ongoing services in Hughes Auditorium over the several days of suspended classes during the revival.

One of the most memorable, life changing, and sustaining events that took place in our lives and family resulted from the 1950 revival. One day during this revival, my father came home saying that he had felt the Lord speaking to him about the need for a change in our family devotions. Up to this point, our family devotions had consisted of reading the *Upper Room*, its scripture and devotional thought for the day, and then praying around our family circle after eating breakfast. My father said that the Lord had impressed upon him that our family of five should begin reading through the Bible, as a family, within a year's time. This would require us to get up about thirty minutes earlier each day, read three chapters a day during the week and five chapters on Sundays. We would each read seven verses aloud and thus complete our reading each day and then pray individually, starting with my father, then the oldest to the youngest child, with our mother closing our prayer time. I participated in this experience for the next ten years until I left home at twenty years of age to live in the dormitory for my senior year at Asbury College.

I cannot describe satisfactorily the deep lasting impact this experience of discipline and exposure to the truth of God's Word has had upon my life and my own family. Today, I cherish God's Word as the inspired, inerrant, and infallible revelation to me, my wife and our family of four children and their spouses and our 15 grandchildren. The Lord's mercies are new every morning and great is His faithfulness to us. The blessings of the 1950 revival at Asbury College continue to be realized in many people's lives to this day to the honor and glory of our Lord Jesus Christ.

Fletcher Anderson – 1950

INTRODUCTION: Students' parents who lived at a distance also came under the spell of God's grace. Rev. Fletcher Anderson, a 1950 graduate, illustrates the point. Fletcher later became a career missionary with OMS, spending a good portion of his career in South America, especially Cuba. Fletcher was 85 years old when he shared the following story of his father's conversion. I relayed this story to a young Asbury student, and I liked her reaction described below.

In 2015, during the 125th anniversary of what is now Asbury University, informal interviews were conducted with current students. In response to the question, "What can you tell me about the Asbury revivals?" the answers were vague. "Not much," was the typical reply.

Two fine college histories[1] aptly fill in the gaps; nevertheless, personal details are generally lacking in comprehensive books of this sort. But student eyes grew wide when they heard specific personal accounts. "I didn't really know something like that happened here." After hearing the following story, related by Fletcher Anderson, a student named Amy exclaimed, "I can't wait to read the book about these revivals!"

"The 1950 Asbury revival (and a similar one at Wheaton) caught the attention of numerous magazines, TV broadcasts, and newspapers around the nation. My family lived in Tampa, Florida. The *Tampa Tribune* covered the story, and my father apparently read it. Up to this point my dad was a 'CE Christian' (Christmas and Easter) at best. When I returned home over spring break, Dad said, 'I read about your school in the news and something clicked. I've found the Lord.' For the remainder of his life, my dad became very involved in his local Methodist church; people took note that he was a changed man. Incidentally, my mother and a friend had prayed nineteen years for my dad's salvation. Talk about joy!"

[1] Joseph A. Thacker, *Asbury College: Vision and Miracle* (Nappanee, IN: Evangel Press, 1990). Edward McKinley, *A Purpose Rare: 125 Years of Asbury University*, Ed Kulaga, ed. (Ann Arbor, MI: Edwards Brothers Malloy, 2015).

Jiles E. Kirkland – 1950

INTRODUCTION: Dr. Jiles Kirkland is a retired United Methodist pastor who resides in Lake Junaluska, North Carolina. Writing 50 years after the events described,[1] Dr. Kirkland provides a comprehensive view of the 1950 revival, as well as a sketch of its impact on numerous churches. This revival was the first Asbury spontaneous revival that overflowed well beyond itself. (Revivals in 1958 and 1970 also involved widespread immediate impact on colleges, churches, and communities.)

The revival of 1950 was a spontaneous visitation of the Holy Spirit in a modern Pentecost which forever altered the lives of hundreds of persons. My wife, Eloise, and I were seniors at Asbury College in 1950. We lived off campus so were not involved in the inner lives of students on campus.

On that winter morning in 1950, we had taken our seats in Hughes Auditorium as usual, expecting a routine chapel experience, although, it should be noted, these services were not always routine. For example, E. Stanley Jones was our guest preacher in my sophomore year. That day he spoke on the text, "One greater than the temple is here." In just a few seconds following the message the altar was filled with students who were earnestly seeking God. The experience carried over into the classrooms, where scores of students witnessed the power of God working in their lives.

That morning in 1950 the student body had gathered and had barely taken their seats before a handsome 6'4" senior, Herbert Van Vorce, jumped to his feet and said that he had a witness to make before God, the faculty, and the entire student body. He told how for four years at Asbury he had lived in rebellion, rejected God, broken every rule, and committed virtually every sin in the book. This, despite the fact that his father was a Methodist preacher, and that he had been in a Christian school.

"It all happened" [his conversion to Christ], Herb said, "in an all-night prayer meeting last night."

We were later to learn that there had been many such late-night prayer meetings going on for weeks on campus. We could sense it. There was something about his witness. All those present were soon to see and feel things they had never before experienced.

Indeed, Herb had barely finished his testimony before several others were on their feet to tell of similar experiences. There was a strange sense of expectancy in the air. After a bit, however, the worship leader was able to move on with his designed service. The speaker of the morning was presented, but everything that he said seemed strangely removed from what was about to happen.

As the service concluded that day, Dean J. B. Kenyon came to the platform and asked us to be seated. We all knew that Dean Kenyon was not naturally an emotional man. But he was clearly moved by the Spirit at that moment. With his voice appearing to break at times, he spoke to us and said, "God has been speaking to me during the service this morning, and I don't want to be disobedient. God has told me that I should give you students an opportunity to say some things that might be on your hearts."

I am sure that no one present was prepared for, or expected, what followed. Students were instantly on their feet all over the auditorium. They formed a line all the way to the narthex, moving one by one to the microphone to unburden their hearts and openly declare their purpose to be right with God and each other. They filled the altar engaging in fervent prayer.

There were confessions of cheating, unkind criticism of others, spiritual pride, prayerlessness, coldness, and trying to follow Christ and the world at the same time. Even the faculty members came forward to confess to the alienations and spiritual deserts in their own souls.

Some spoke with choked emotion, but most of those who shared were strangely subdued. Yet, they were plainly stirred to the depths and were utterly sincere. This went on for 72 hours plus, as an unbroken succession of students moved to the platform to speak of the Holy Spirit moving in their lives.

Classes were not canceled,[2] but for days there was no attempt to check attendance. It was truly a visitation of Pentecost which would mark, for eternity, all of us who shared in it.

Soon the press was on campus, and once they began to tell the story, word spread across America. Visitors came from near and far, and many of them experienced life-changing encounters with the living God.

Students and faculty were being implored by pastors and congregations in many states to come and share with them the glory of God happening. As the second weekend of the revival started, I was invited to preach in a youth revival at the First Methodist Church in Florence, Kentucky. After I preached on Friday night, the altar was flooded with young people. The same occurred on Saturday night. I preached at the Sunday morning worship service. When I gave the invitation, people streamed to the altar and were kneeling literally six or seven deep. The service went until 2:00 p.m.

Sunday evening found the sanctuary filled again and many earnest seekers once more lined the altar. The people said, "We can't stop now! Can you stay longer?" While I protested that I had to get back to classes, I did agree to preach for the next two nights. We had conversions at all the services. Whole families were united in Christ.

This same story was repeated in church after church where students went to share the story of the 1950 winter Pentecost at Asbury.

---

[1]"Jiles Kirkland," *Memories of Asbury Revival of 1950,* Marion L. Walker, ed., pp. 44-46. AUA.

[2]Correction: classes were eventually officially dismissed, though the record is mixed on how long. See "Isaac Patton," *Memories of Asbury Revival 1950,* p. 29; Joseph A. Thacker Jr., *Asbury College: Vision and Miracle,* p. 201.

The Class Play that Never Was. During the revival of 1950, each student who rose to speak came and stood in front of Hughes Auditorium in front of a velvet curtain drawn before a stage set for the Junior Class play, "Our Hearts were Young and Gay." The play, scheduled to be given Friday and Saturday night by the Junior Class, was postponed indefinitely because of the revival. AUA

A Financial Success. The Junior Class play was to have been a fund-raiser to remodel Hughes Auditorium, but the play was never performed. One year later Dean Kenyon decided simply to pass the hat instead. When the offering was tabulated, the proceeds exceeded the fondest expectations of the play sponsors. AUA

Compared to Baseball. "We have no apologies to make. We have found God anew.... We may, at times, make a lot of noise, but don't let that bother you. I've heard a lot more noise at a ball game when the batter strikes out. And in here we have the biggest strike out of them all." *Dean Kenyon.* AUA

Revival or War? "Reflecting [*on the student spiritual awakening*], the thought occurred to me that perhaps more of this is the answer to the war-wracked world." *1950, Lexington Newspaperman.* AUA

The Devil's Get Well Card. One student injected some humor into a testimony. "I ought to send the devil a get well card, since he's probably sick today. The devil has given me a hard time and I'm glad to be giving him a hard one now." AUA

No Pride Allowed. President Z. T. Johnson said, "There is no feeling of elation or boasting on the part of us at Asbury College. We feel honored to have had such a gracious outpouring and to have found the favor of the Lord." AUA

Tony M. Anderson – 1950

INTRODUCTION: In 2000, Marion L. Walker, now deceased, completed an unpublished collection of reflections by some participants in the 1950 revival. About three quarters of Marion's own reflections revolve around Reverend Dr. Tony M. Anderson.[1] Portions of Anderson's story appear in Halls Aflame, *by Henry James and Paul A. Rader. Everyone was in awe of Dr. Anderson.*

Early in January 1950, a group of students at Asbury College had a burden for a mighty revival and also for a senior student, Herb Van Vorce, who was unsaved.

Around that time, a professor, Dr. Tony M. Anderson, probably one of the greatest evangelists the Nazarene Church ever produced, woke shortly after midnight. These are his words: "I looked at the clock and said, 'It's not time to get up.' The Lord spoke to me and said, 'What about giving me some time?' Now I was not backslid, but I said, 'I read my Bible and pray.' I was very busy preaching every weekend, preaching all summer long in camp meetings, holding revivals during the school year, writing books, and teaching school. I was almost seventy years old, literally almost on the verge of a nervous collapse. I sat for three or four hours that morning in my room and cried and prayed. I told the Lord, 'You can have all of me, if I never teach another class, or preach another sermon, or write another book. You can have all of me.' The Lord renewed me to the point that sometimes after that I only got two or three hours of sleep at night. I don't know what it is to be tired. That first morning, I said, 'Lord, I am approaching seventy years, the allotted time. I would love to see one great revival before I die.' Every morning I got up early around 4:00 a.m. and prayed for several hours for a revival while the students had this vigil of prayer going."

The next morning in chapel a couple got up and sang, "Let me lose my life and find it Lord in Thee." There was a scheduled speaker, but he only spoke briefly. The atmosphere just seemed to be electrified with the presence of the Lord. A student named Bob Barefoot got up and said that he had just been in an all-night prayer meeting in the gym, and a student, for whom we had been praying, Herb Van Vorce, had been converted. At that point, Herb Van Vorce himself jumped up and said, "I am that student. I was about to graduate from Asbury without God." Several students came to the altar. Dr. Anderson got up and said, "I wish for one day around here, just one day, we could forget about school, and everything else, and let God have His way."

Then it broke out. Students started going to the altar.

All of the basketball players from the local high school came to the chapel and were saved. Also a group of ministerial students from Campbellsville Baptist College, in Campbellsville, Kentucky, drove all night to get there. They arrived at 4:00 a.m. They said, "We heard about the revival, and we want to find out about it. We want to know about the doctrine you teach called Entire Sanctification." The Asbury student replied, "Here's the man you want to talk to: Dr. T. M. Anderson." Dr. Anderson, who had just walked in, said, "I have a classroom down in the basement of Hughes Auditorium. Let's go down to my classroom." Once they were there, Dr. Anderson said, "Now you are ministerial students. You have been saved and called to preach. We teach that after you are converted, you are to be filled with the Holy Spirit, which we call sanctification. The only thing I know is that you have to pray for it." All of those boys fell down on their knees and began to pray God would fill them with the Holy Ghost and sanctify them wholly. Most, if not all, were filled with the Holy Ghost and were sanctified.

The students spread out and began witnessing. One student phoned his millionaire mother in Jackson, Mississippi, and asked if he could fly down and bring some students for a Wednesday night prayer meeting. She said, "Yes, get them on the plane and bring them down." So a group of students flew to Jackson. The next morning the students called Dr. Anderson. "We gave our testimony last night and started an all night prayer meeting. We had 200 people at the altar. What do you think that we should do next?" These students had the stewardess on her knees praying. They testified on the airplane to Bob Feller, who was the pitcher with the famous Cleveland Indians.

About ten days later, Dr. Anderson and more students flew down to Jackson, the capital of Mississippi. When they arrived, the state legislature was ready to convene. They sent word to Dr. Anderson and asked if he would come over and open the Senate with prayer. Would he also have a student go over and open the House with prayer? Dr. Anderson replied that he didn't have a prayer written out. They, in turn, said that they didn't want him to read a prayer, they wanted him just to pray. Dr. Anderson prayed like he was in a campmeeting. The legislators shook his hand and told Dr. Anderson that they appreciated his prayer. They hadn't heard anything quite like that in all their lives.

A Baptist preacher called Dr. Anderson—a Nazarene Evangelist—to come to his church for a service. This was a large church of about eight hundred people. It was 9:00 p.m. when Dr. Anderson got up to preach. "Listen to this. Do you remember the story of Paul when he preached a long time? A fellow went to sleep. He fell out of a window and was killed. Paul went down to him and revived him. Paul brought him back up." When Dr. Anderson was finished, it was 3:00 a.m. He said that he was tired and tried to quit preaching, but the people wouldn't let him.

The Lord gave Dr. Anderson some deep insights and special knowledge that proved he was a great blessing to many people.

One morning he said to his class, "Do you young ladies in here know of a Miss Hill on campus?" Dr. Anderson didn't know her. All he knew was her last name. The students replied, "Yes, we know her. She lives in our dormitory." Dr. Anderson told the students, "You tell her that I said that I saw her running away from God, and that she should be very careful." The students went and told Miss Hill. She became very angry and went to Dr. Anderson's home enraged. He said to her, "It's true, you have been running away from God. By the way, I see you in your hometown. You are at a party pouring drinks."

"Oh, no, Dr. Anderson, you can't know that! Nobody does!"

"It's true isn't it?" Dr. Anderson asked.

Miss Hill fell on her knees and began to pray. Dr. Anderson said that he saw God strike her. That was the word that he used. She jumped up from the floor and was gloriously converted.

Dr. Anderson said, "When you go home between semesters, there is a young lady who is an associate of yours. You will have the privilege of leading her to Christ."

Miss Hill cried, "Oh no, Dr. Anderson, I have already damned her life." But Miss Hill went home and led her friend to Christ. She was converted.

Dr. Anderson went to a revival meeting in Texas. He got up around 3:30 in the morning to pray. At 4:00 a.m. two men knocked on his door. One of the men told Dr. Anderson a long, sad story. Dr. Anderson looked at him and said, "That is not your problem. Your problem is that you are running around and fooling around with a little red-headed woman down here. If you don't leave her alone, you will die and go to hell." God had told Dr. Anderson this before the men arrived. Some people were afraid to go near Dr. Anderson for fear of what he might know about them.

I knew Dr. Anderson. I was one of his students at Asbury College. I lived next door to him and was often in his home.

One day, I was on my way to the Wilmore Campmeeting. Clay Milby was the song leader for the Central Holiness Camp-meeting in Wilmore. Before he went to the afternoon service of the campmeeting, Clay stopped in to visit Dr. Anderson. Dr. Anderson was on the phone when Clay got there. When Dr. Anderson finished his phone conversation, he said that he was talking long distance to a Nazarene preacher's wife in Tennessee. Then Dr. Anderson told this story, "I was in Tennessee holding a revival for a pastor who limped. I knew the pastor wasn't too well. I got up the next morning at 4:00 and sat down on the side of the bed to pray because my knees were too sore to kneel. The Savior came. I saw a vision of the pastor. The Savior walked over to the pastor and turned him around. The Savior pulled up the pastor's shirt, exposing his back. At the base of his spinal column was a four inch hole. There were four inches of his backbone missing. I jumped off the bed and asked the Lord to touch the pastor's back, but the Lord didn't. That morning at breakfast I said to the pastor, 'Is there four inches of your backbone missing?' He replied, 'Yes, the doctors x-rayed it and it is missing.' I asked him, 'How do you live?' He said, 'I don't know.'" Dr. Anderson said, "I saw a black streak going down the back of your leg. Do you mind if I tell the congregation tonight?" The pastor replied, 'No, it's true.'"

So that night at the Nazarene Church, Dr. Anderson said, "We are going to pray for your pastor." Dr. Anderson then told them of their pastor's condition. "We are going to kneel down at the altar and pray for him. I also want to tell you that there are a bunch of you who have been in church for many years who have not been sanctified. I don't want a single one of you down here praying for your pastor. I want you to pray for yourself to get sanctified." The people fell all over the church praying.

The next morning when Dr. Anderson was praying, he had a vision of the pastor again. The Savior walked in, exposed the pastor's back. This time the Savior put his hand over the hole. When he removed his hand, the hole was closed with a light radiating around it.

Since that time the pastor's wife told Dr. Anderson that her husband had not one pain since then and was preaching like a house on fire.

From then on, Dr. Anderson said that his whole concept of revival changed. He said that he had pastors call asking, "Dr. Anderson, won't you come and hold a revival? You won't have to worry about a thing. We have money for you. All we want is for you to come." Dr. Anderson replied that he wasn't interested in their money. Unless they were willing to start an all-night prayer meeting, he was not going. God gave him some powerful and great revivals after that.

Dr. Anderson had an unsaved son. He told Z. T. Johnson, President of the college, "Jesus has told me that my son is going to be saved." Dr. Johnson said, "Well, I would be a little careful to talk like that." Sure enough, Dr. Anderson's son was saved. Many people were healed, saved, and delivered.

[1]Marion Walker, "Isaac Patton," *Memories of the Asbury Revival of 1950*, pp. 4-5, 8-14.

- Widespread media exposure (including television).

- Coincidence of the Wheaton revival, which drew attention and a news article from *Time Magazine*

- Many teams went out to share, and the revival spread widely to churches and other institutions of higher learning. Revivals in 1958 and 1970 followed suit.

Racial Relations. It is rather speculative, but at least one research-er raised the issue of racial segregation as it relates to revivals at southern colleges. How might this intersect with worship styles and witnessing endeavors? After the Second World War, barriers to racial integration were challenged and began to erode. Even so, LTC Melvin Bowdan, Jr. USA, Asbury's first African American professor, administrator, and member of the Board of Trustees, noted that as late as 1970 he found no record of a witness team going to a historically black college or African American congregation. In more recent times there have been strong efforts to increase racial diversity in most southern institutions of higher learning. Asbury is among them. See also Edward McKinley, *A Purpose Rare*, pp. 136-137.

Paul Rader – 1958, 2006

INTRODUCTION: Dr. Paul A. Rader was a seminary student in 1958. Building upon an unpublished account by Henry James, Paul coauthored the book Halls Aflame *(1966). It was the first book published about an Asbury revival, the second being* One Divine Moment *(1970). Dr. Rader provides other biographical references in his personal story below. We should mention that when he retired as The Salvation Army General (the first American to hold this international office), he almost immediately assumed the presidency of Asbury from 2000 to 2006. There were notable achievements during his administration. Among them are a graduate program in education, the Highbridge Film Festival, and the recruitment of more international and minority students. After leaving the presidency he helped secure a grant to construct the Andrew S. Miller Center for Communication Arts.*

Remembering the Move of the Spirit...

The campus and community of Asbury College were still reveling in the afterglow of the powerful 1950 revival when I arrived as a freshman in the fall of 1952. A sister and brother had preceded me, touching down in the fall of 1950, and were keenly aware of the impact of the Spirit's work during those days and weeks of awakening. Many students who had lived through those days were still on campus. The flames may have abated in some degree, but there was a pervasive scent in the air redolent of revival. It was evident in the ready response and fervency of prayer at the long altar in Hughes Auditorium that was often crowded with seekers at the end of chapel hours, without the need for pressure or pleading by preachers of the hour. The fall and winter revivals were also powerful times of renewal. Faculty reflected the reality of the Spirit's refreshing. We were all more sensitive to the Spirit than we may ever have been. One professor in a chapel prayer memorably spoke of our sense of awe at the "stately steppings of the Spirit" among us. The tragic deaths of two of the leaders in the 1950 Revival, Bob Barefoot and Bill Ruether, seemed in some way to be the price of Satan's humiliation.

By 1958 I had moved on to Asbury Seminary and was in my middler year. There was a quiet and intentional prayer movement that laid the ground for the outpouring of the Spirit that broke upon the college campus in the spring of that year. Professor Leon Fisher was the speaker in chapel, centering a challenging message on 2 Corinthians 13:5, "Examine yourselves to see if you are in the faith. Test yourselves!" Professor Fisher was an able and engaging preacher, but not at all bombastic or overly emotional in his presentation. But it was God's moment. The Spirit came upon us. A student leader went to the pulpit asking to speak. He poured his heart out in confession of hypocrisy, pleading for forgiveness. Others followed. The altar filled with a wave of tearful seekers. Students lined up at the pulpit for the chance to voice their soul agony and desire for pardon and cleansing. To my memory, classes were canceled for that day. But it was only the beginning.

Even when classes resumed, the revival burned on. Day after day and all through the night, there were students filling the auditorium. There was some exhortation by faculty and staff, but the movement was Spirit-led. The word went out, and as with earlier awakenings, students came from other schools and churches to witness what God was doing on the Asbury campus, carrying the flame back with them on their return. To my memory, the revival did not have anything like the impact on the seminary campus that it had on the college. I have never been sure why. There were, of course, many of us who, on hearing of God's dealings with the college, soon made our way across to Hughes Auditorium, not wanting to miss out on the blessing. I will never forget a powerful witness of the Spirit that came to my heart when returning to the seminary campus from sharing in the vital sense of God's presence in Hughes. We know what we know through our faith in the Word. But sometimes God in His grace grants us such an awareness of His indwelling presence and power that all doubt or uncertainty is swept aside and our hearts are aglow with a glory and certainty that cannot be denied.

Only heaven will reveal the fruit of that movement of the Spirit. It did not, I think, reach as widely as the 1950 revival or the 1970 revival, but for those whom it touched it was life-changing. Who can know what part it played in commitments to lifelong service on the frontiers of mission? We bow our heads in deep gratitude as we remember the gift of those days and hours.

Following this time of revival, Henry James, a fellow student who had published an account of the 1950 Revival, asked me to join him in updating and revising the earlier book while adding a new section on the 1958 awakening. This account of the revivals is entitled *Halls Aflame*.

Kay and I were serving in Korea as Salvation Army missionary officers when the fire fell on the Asbury campus in 1970. Word soon reached us in excited phone calls telling of the powerful working of the Spirit on campus. The 1970 revival had a broad reach across the nation and beyond. A Baptist missionary colleague came to see us, excitedly relating to us the impact of the revival on the campus of Southwestern Baptist Seminary. A group of Asbury students had visited the Southwestern campus to share what God was doing. They stood up on a table in the dining hall and began to speak. Our friend told of the instant and dramatic response of students as the story of the revival was simply shared. The flame of revival swept across the campus. One New Testament professor later spoke of how the encounter with the Asbury students and the movement of the Spirit that followed caused him to consider the person and work of the Holy Spirit in a way he had never done before. His teaching was apparently revolutionized. So the impact of what happened across the globe was felt in our missionary community in Korea, as it must have done in other fields, as well.

Students launched out across the country as informal witnesses all aglow with the spirit of revival. Kay's brother, Jim Fuller, now a professor and dean at Indiana Wesleyan University, joined with a fellow student to form a team they dubbed "Jim 'n I"! They had no planned itinerary, but followed what they felt to be the Spirit's leading. They moved from community to community, speaking in churches, schools, and anywhere they could gather a crowd. They traveled by motorcycle, riding across the nation to California and back. Others found unique opportunities to spread the fire, as well.

We returned to the States for advanced study at Fuller Seminary School of World Mission in 1971. The next year I was invited to preach the regularly scheduled college revival. In fact, true revival, the likes of the 1950, 1958 and 1970 years, cannot be scheduled or orchestrated. It is God's sovereign gift to his Church when it occurs. As the great evangelist, Charles G. Finney maintained, however, in his *Lectures on Revival*, God moves his people by the Spirit to employ means through which revival characteristically occurs. In each case of the moving of the Spirit in such powerful ways, one can be assured that in anticipation of such spiritual breakthrough, prayer warriors have been chosen to shoulder a deep burden of intercession—often with confession on behalf of the people, as with the Old Testament prophets. Someone, somewhere, somehow is carrying the burden and exercising conquering faith for an outpouring of the Spirit. So while Asbury College faithfully programmed regular revival seasons, which were greatly honored of the Lord and bore lasting fruit for the Kingdom, they differed in extent and impact from the major movings of God's Spirit we have had in view. Having said that, even two years later, we rejoiced in the warmth and power of the Spirit's presence and the "Sweet, Sweet Spirit" in that place, which we knew to be authentically the Spirit of the Lord, in the words of the chorus sung so often during the 1970 Revival.

CONCLUSION: Dr. Rader was President during the most recent spontaneous revival in 2006. His comments related to that occasion comprise a postcript near the close of this anthology.

Eldon and Agnes Niehof – 1958

INTRODUCTION: Rev. Dr. Eldon and Agnes Niehof are long-term leaders associated with the Kentucky Mountain Holiness Institute (KMHI), founded in 1926 by Lela McConnell. Eldon was nominated to take Dr. McConnell's place as president of KMHI in 1966. Eldon and Agnes presently reside in retirement close to the KMHI headquarters in eastern Kentucky.

I was a junior at Asbury College in 1958. We were in the 8:00 a.m. chapel on a Saturday. Professor Leon Fisher was the speaker. At the close of chapel, Art Osborn, a member of the Junior Class, went to the platform and asked to speak. He had been the president of our Sophomore Class. He told of his own spiritual need and disappointment at Asbury. He said he was going to the altar and invited others that were like him to join him. The aisles immediately filled with students making their way to the altar. Others prayed with the seekers. As students prayed through they went to the platform and testified. This went on all morning. There were no classes. Only one person left chapel to go to the dining hall at noon.

I and others pastored churches some distance from Wilmore in Kentucky, Ohio, and Indiana. We had to leave, but the revival continued around the clock with people seeking at the altar, testifying from the pulpit on the platform, and sitting in the congregation. I arrived back on campus on Monday morning and this had continued non-stop.

Agnes, my girl friend who later became my wife, was also a member of the Junior Class at Asbury at that time. She did not go with me to my pastoral assignment. She remained at the college and was in the chapel for much of Saturday and Sunday.

NOTE: Agnes reflects on her experience:

The presence of the Lord was rich in Hughes Auditorium. Many young people lined up to share their testimonies and told how the Lord was speaking to them. Many continued to seek the Lord and stayed.

Several alumni from Kentucky Mountain Bible Institute were students at Asbury at that time. Two of those, Grace and Ruth Davis, joined the line in the front of Hughes. Grace felt they should sing "Glory to Jesus." The Lord settled down in an unusual way as they sang. The service continued all night long.

Some had to leave and go to their church appointments on Sunday morning, and others had to go to their evening appointments. They told about the unusual move of the Lord at Asbury. God used them to reach the hearts of many in these churches. I went with a group to a mission church in nearby Nicholasville, Kentucky. We, too, felt that an unusual presence of the Lord came with us. We returned to Asbury where the revival was still in progress.

On Sunday many witnessed in churches throughout the area, in jails, and on the phone. The power of God was felt everywhere they went. I was back in Hughes Auditorium in the afternoon and evening on Monday and people continued to pray at the altar and testify.

Students from the seminary came to witness what was happening. God's presence was real and filling the place. When visitors came and stepped inside they sensed the unusual presence of God.

On Monday evening President Dr. Z. T. Johnson came to the auditorium and announced that the revival would continue at the Methodist Church with Dr. Tony Anderson preaching. Classes began as usual on Tuesday, but praying at the altar continued night and day for much if not all of the following week.

This mighty outpouring of the Spirit was the result of prayer and fasting over a period of time. Each Thursday at noon there was a fast prayer meeting where faculty, staff, and students met to pray. The effects of this revival made a tremendous difference in the atmosphere of the campus.

SNAPSHOT
The Varied and Changing Meanings of the Word "Revival"

Comments by a Bishop in India in 1964. In ecumenical circles today there seems to be a distaste for the word "revival" and a preference for its synonym "renewal." Why is this? To the people in the British Commonwealth—including India but excluding Canada—the word "revival" denotes a "renewed interest in religion after indifference or decline, a period of religious awakening," which is Webster's first definition.... The word "revival" recalls the stirring days of the White-field-Wesley movement, or the Second Great Awakening of 1859, or the Welsh Revival of 1904. In the minds of Americans, the word "revival" primarily means human promotion; but to the *Commonwealth* Christians, it primarily means Divine visitation. A. J. Appasamy, *Write the Vision!: J. Edwin Orr's Thirty Years of Adventurous Service*, p. 222.

Balcony View of Worshippers, 1950

Student Witness Team Departure, 1970

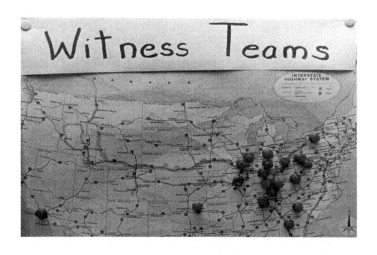

Early Map Student Witness Team Destinations, 1970

Jeannine Brabon - 1970

INTRODUCTION: Dr. Dennis Kinlaw wrote a preface to a workbook companion to the 2001 edition of The Wesley Great Experiment: A Life that Really Matters.

> "I rejoice that a new edition is being produced. We sometimes forget the power of a book or a simple pamphlet that has a revolutionary idea in it. That came home to me in 1970 when it was my privilege to experience the most remarkable movement of the Spirit of God that it has been my opportunity to see. In the fall of 1969 there were a number of students, a third year girl in particular, who found their hearts moved with a concern for their fellow students and for the college. They found a little booklet that challenged them—it spoke of what we now know as The Wesley Great Experiment. That fall six students committed themselves to each other and to God to see what difference it would make in their lives...."[1]

The "third-year" student was Jeannine Brabon. Here is her story. Born into a missionary family in Colombia in 1949, Jeannine Brabon learned to lean on God from birth. "I grew up in the persecuted church."

This included threats of violence, kidnapping and even death. "I received a call to become a missionary at age eleven. I felt inadequate for God's call on my life. I knew I might be called to lay down my life. My hunger for God led me to surrender all and to let the Holy Spirit fill me. I entered into an intimate walk with Jesus. In high school, I was challenged to pray more. How? I was in a regimented boarding school. The Holy Spirit impressed me to pray every hour. I took 3x5 cards for every hour in the day, a set for each day in the week. It took me two months to organize but it became a lifelong habit."

She matriculated at Asbury in August 1967 and sensed a spiritual drought on campus. There was an administrative upheaval, including a rancorous campaign to remove a recalcitrant college President. She felt she had two options, "You can either criticize or pray." Rather than sign a student petition to oust the President, Jeannine felt the Holy Spirit calling her to pray. Students and faculty appeared on her prayer cards. An observer related, "She would pray while waiting in line at the cafeteria. Never an idle moment." Shy by nature, she was elected Class Chaplain in her junior year.

The atmosphere on campus improved under Dr. Kinlaw's able skills, but latent faculty tensions and student discontent smoldered like a partially spent forest fire. It was the height of the Viet Nam War and the counterculture movement; rural campuses were not immune to illegal drug use. Many students felt treated like children versus young adults, and they pushed against rules like curfews and hair length. A vocal minority expressed dismay at apparent apathy about the war and racial integration. Asbury needed a touch from God, and Jeannine knew it.

In 1968 she went to work. She posted a sign COME APART TO PRAY on a classroom door. A handful of people met in the basement of Hughes Auditorium for a half hour before each chapel. Other unnamed student prayer groups were meeting on campus.

At a weekly fast prayer meeting in 1969, a student stated, "I wish we could pray all night." Jeannine requested permission to hold an all-night service on Friday, October 3. She walked into Hughes Auditorium a little before midnight and turned on the skylights.

"'God, show me that all I've prayed up till now, I know nothing about prayer.' I was jubilant when one hundred fifty students appeared, including a dozen male students. We sat in groups interceding. The Shekinah glory fell."

About 3 a.m. Dr. Hunter, the only professor present, found Jeannine seated in the balcony. He said, "I am trying to find out who is in charge here." She replied, "Dr. Hunter, I believe it is the Holy Spirit." He said, "Well, don't you think He has met us?" She responded, "Yes, let's go down and thank Him." The eighty students who lasted through the night gathered in a circle to pray.

The next morning a student cornered Jeannine after eight o'clock chapel. "Nothing happened in chapel this morning." Jeannine asked if the girl had ever read Acts 1:7. "It is not for you to know times or seasons which the Father has put in His own authority. But you shall receive power when the Holy Spirit has come upon you; and you shall be witnesses to Me in Jerusalem, and in all Judea and Samaria, and to the end of the earth." Jeannine said, "God is coming, in His time."

Earlier in January the Spirit of God percolated during a series of scheduled services at the Wilmore United Methodist Church. Singer Doug Oldham bared his heart by saying that he was faking it and needed to get right with God. People poured to the altar. The scheduled speaker never preached. It was a foretaste of what was yet to come.

There was one final development, an earlier initiative coming to full fruition. Jeannine and five other students had begun a slightly modified version of the thirty-day *Wesley Great Experiment* in the autumn with some leaders. The second cycle began in January with thirty additional student leaders. These students shared their experiences in chapel on January 31. The hope was to get students into a disciplined walk with God. The response was overwhelming. By Monday, February 2, two hundred students had responded. When revival came God had His follow-up plan ready.

The moment had arrived. On February 3, light snow was falling during the 10 a.m. chapel. Sensing that there was something in the air, Jeannine leaned toward her chapel partner whispering, "I have a test next hour."

She responded, "So do I, but I don't think we'll take them." Academic Dean Custer Reynolds had a decision to make; should he extend the service or resume classes? Eddie Bonniwell nudged Jeannine, "Go tell him this cannot stop." She said, "You go." Eddie and Dr. Hunter reached Dr. Reynolds on stage about the same time with the same message, "Let the Spirit's work continue." God tipped the balance. Dr. Reynolds announced, "Class is cancelled." The heavens burst forth and ushered in an unforgettable week in God's presence.

Jeannine returned to Colombia as a missionary with OMS International. Among other activities, she became heavily involved in prison ministry at Bellavista Prison. Here is a little known story.

> Medellin, Colombia, was one the most violent cities in the world....In 1975, the Bellavista Prison was built to help control the ever-growing violence, but the violence soon controlled the prison. The war on the streets continued inside the walls. On average there were fifty murders a month, and sometimes, as many as twenty deaths a day. Bellavista became one of the most violent prisons in the world.
>
> The day Jesus was lifted up as the only solution, the deaths abruptly stopped. A church and a Bible Institute were started inside Bellavista. The world's most vicious criminals began turning away from their evil ways. Inmates' lives and the prison were radically transformed. In the past 16 years, there have only been fifteen deaths inside Bellavista.
>
> Now Bellavista is the least violent prison in all of Latin America. The men who were once the cause of the violence now run the prison ministry.[2]

CONCLUSION: Is there any link between Asbury and Bellavista Prison? I like to think that Dr. Kinlaw would smile and say, "I have a sneaking suspicion the answer is yes."

God continues to use Jeannine. Besides an honorary doctor of Christian Ministries degree from Asbury University, she received the World Methodist Council Peace Award in 2009.

"This award, the highest given by the Methodist/Wesleyan family from around the world, is given annually to individuals or groups who have, through their courage, creativity, and consistency, made significant contributions to peace, justice, and reconciliation. What is most important for Jeannine is that Jesus Christ be lifted up and glorified in her life." [3]

[1]Teague, Sam E., *The Wesley Great Experience: Surrendering to the Spirit* (Franklin, TN: Providence House, 2001), p. 3

[2]*The Untold Stories of Colombia*, DVD (One Mission International, 2007), Jacket Cover. YouTube presentation at www.youtube.com/watch?v=0is4duEqvEs (accessed 1/22/16).

[3]One Mission Society, https://onemissionsociety.org/give/jeanninebrabon (accessed 4/1/16).

THE JOHN WESLEY GREAT EXPERIMENT
Wanted: Ten Brave Christians[1]

INTRODUCTION: People wonder about the John Wesley Great Experiment *(also known as* "The Wesley Experience")*, including how it began and what it involves. It came in rapid-fire response to a heartfelt prayer by Sam Teague in 1965. Some would say it was anointed, and indeed God has used it in the lives of many people. About three dozen students adopted it preceding the 1970 revival. Jeannine Brabon's story elucidates some of the details. One correction is in order. In places we read that two hundred students were utilizing the* Wesley Experiment *guidelines before the 1970 Revival began. But careful research reveals that this wider group signed cards to use a modified form of the plan while they were in chapel on Saturday, January 31, three days before the floodgates of heaven opened. Of course, this widespread openness to use basic spiritual disciplines deepened and leavened everything else that followed. Like the early church at Pentecost, God prepared a core to sustain all that followed (see Acts, Chapters 1-2).*

"Dear God, show me the way to motivate these young people to build a life that matters."

After praying that simple prayer, Sam Teague, the leader of the Christian Home Builders Sunday School Class at John Wesley Methodist Church in Tallahassee, Florida, felt a deep stirring within.

He said: "Suddenly, I sat up and began to write. I wrote furiously for the ideas came to me clearly and with certainty. When I started writing it was about 9:00 AM—when I finished writing it was 9:20 AM. In twenty minutes God had written through my hand the entire program of *The Ten Brave Christians*."[2]

The best explanation of the profound impact of this challenge upon individuals, groups, and churches is that it came as God's answer to prayer. Below is the gist of the challenge.

WANTED: Ten Brave Christians Who, For One Month, Will...

1. Meet once a week to learn how to pray;

2. Work at least two hours in the church each week and do a daily good deed (self surrender);

3 Give God one-tenth of your earnings (self denial);

4 Spend from 5:30 to 6:00 each morning in prayer and study of Scripture (self control);

5 Witness about your experience with God to others.

Study these five principles carefully so there is no misunderstanding as to what is involved in surrendering your life to God. Here is the commitment you make now:

To prepare my life to receive from God the great strength and power available through prayer, I ask to become a member of this group_____.[3]

[1]Danny Morris and Sam Teague, *The John Wesley Great Experiment: The Story of the*

John Wesley Great Experiment (Franklin, TN: Providence House Publishers, 2001).

[2]Teague, *The Wesley Great Experience: Surrendering to the Spirit,* p. 4.

[3]*Ibid.,* p. 7.

NOTE: *[A companion workbook may be procured by contacting: online at - Seedbed.com, by mail at - 415 Bridge St., Franklin, TN 37064, by phone at - 614 442-8582.]*

Lincoln Stevens – 1970

INTRODUCTION: Dr. Lincoln Stevens graduated in 1971, completed a Ph.D. in Philosophy, and in 1977 began his career as a professor at Mount Vernon Nazarene University in Ohio. The following account first appeared as an attachment to a doctoral dissertation by Dr. Phillip Bruce Collier.[1]

Lincoln's story highlights some frequent aspects of Asbury revivals: a sense of God's almost tangible presence, emotions ranging from heart-wrenching contrition to otherworldly calm, relative indifference to eating and sleeping, open confession of sin, bold displays of restitution, divinely engineered coincidences, and a desire to tell others what God has done.

The 1970 Asbury revival began in a normal chapel on February 3. The Academic Dean invited testimonies from students after giving his own. At the end of the chapel Dr. Clarence Hunter said that he believed the altar should be opened for students to respond. In a rush the altar filled with students, four and five deep.

The prayer at the altar was quiet at first, but at times the weeping of deep repentance could be heard. The chapel period was over but no one seemed to move. That was 10:50 AM. Testimonies and confession continued through another hour, and then two. Then it was lunch time but still no one moved. I went to the dining hall and only a handful of people were there.

Dr. Hunter became the informal leader on the podium, and Dr. Paul Roher became the informal song leader. Sometimes songs would break out spontaneously. By evening people began to come from off-campus to see, with some later reporting they were overcome with conviction for sin *as they came* on campus. The congregation swelled to capacity by day and shrank to about 200 some nights. On Friday, February 6, the entire auditorium was overflowing with standing room only. It was a glorious time.

The revival showed me several things. First, God may manifest Himself in a public presence something like the Shekinah Glory of God in the Old Testament. His presence in those days was like an unseen "objective reality" so clearly and fearfully known to us who were there that it was difficult to avoid thinking about Christ and one's relationship to Him, as well as to respond to Him.

The Presence of God was so public and so "thick" that some students went so far as to join forces against responding to Christ, making pacts not to go to Hughes Auditorium *[NOTE: apparently to little avail]* where His presence was centered. Others would awaken from sleep and rush to the altar to find Christ. God was so real that people began to discover that what had been a largely formal or intellectual faith was nothing in light of the Living Presence of God encountered in those places.

In some of the quieter times in the middle of the night, students made their way into the auditorium and to the altar to seek the Lord. In one such case a student stood at the podium reporting the concern of his heart that one of his roommates would find the Lord. That very roommate walked into the auditorium and headed straight to the altar. The student speaking was visibly moved and left the podium to pray with his roommate.

Second, God's presence clearly spread as people went on witness teams *[NOTE: By request or divine direction]* to numerous parts of the United States over the following weeks. The first weekend of the revival perhaps 600 out of 1,000 students traveled off campus witnessing in churches and colleges.

I participated in one witness team to Trevecca Nazarene College. The same powerful Presence overflowed in a similar way in five different church services in Nashville. The normally organized services, after simple testimonies from Asbury students, turned into multiple-hour services.

After those Sunday evening church services, our team of Asbury witnesses met for singing and prayer with some Trevecca students in a boys' dormitory. While we met, three male students literally burst into the room, sobbing uncontrollably, and threw themselves onto the floor. They prayed and were counseled until they were assured of their salvation. We were told later that the three were the most identifiably rebellious students on campus and that they were in their room two floors away from us when they fell under conviction.

Third, the reality of God is more than most of us believe is possible. On a personal level, I found forgiveness and peace in God through Christ that goes beyond emotion and intellect, something that I had never known before. Let me explain. Up to that time I had committed myself several times to God at altar services. But I found myself identifying my spiritual life with the way I felt. When I felt good I thought my relationship with God was right, and when I felt bad I thought my relationship with God was wrong.

I struggled with that cycle of emotionalism through my first two years at Asbury. When the revival began I found myself extremely unhappy, wanting lasting certainty concerning my relationship with Christ. I listened to the continuous testimonies in the auditorium, and even knelt at the altar one time to seek the Lord. But nothing seemed to answer my need. On Saturday morning, February 7, I found what I was looking for.

I returned to the altar again to seek the Lord. Providentially, Rev. Harold Spann came to counsel with me at the altar. He said that it would be good for me to turn to Christ, acknowledge my sins, and confess them to the two people who were around me there at the altar, asking God on the merit of Christ to forgive and cleanse me.

One by one I called from memory sins I had committed and prayed out loud to God. These sins I had largely forgotten, and to this day they are ones that I would not want to mention in public. Somewhere in the middle of this process I received a complete peace regarding my sins. The list of remembered sins had not been completely confessed orally, but God inwardly touched me with His peace. It was an inner knowledge that my sins had been forgiven. It is remarkable to me that through the entire experience I felt no emotion. Since then I have felt many emotions about this and other things I know God has done for me and others, but this experience was not emotion-based at all.

Fourth, 1970 taught me about the power available to transform lives. Relationships among faculty, students, administrators, and families that had been torn or severed for years were healed by the presence of Christ. Some students were very angry over campus rules; they expressed repentance, publicly asked for forgiveness, then made their way to the Dean and threw arms of love around him. An administrator publicly confessed judgmental attitudes toward students and asked for forgiveness.

Over the years, I have never been able to get away from the almost unbelievable spiritual possibilities available in this kind of visitation of Christ. I have often wondered whether the real solution for present-day problems is in the kind of touch from Christ many experienced at Asbury in 1970. I wonder if He will come in this way again, perhaps with an even more widespread impact. My belief is that we desperately need it; my hope and prayer is that He will.

[1]Phillip Bruce Collier, "The Significance of the Asbury College Revival of 1970 for Some Aspects of the Spiritual Lives of the Participants." *A Dissertation Presented to the Faculty of Asbury Theological Seminary in Partial Fulfillment of the Requirements for the Degree of Doctor of Ministry,* May 1995, pp. 175-179.

Mark Nysewander – 1970

INTRODUCTION: While serving as Executive Director of the Francis Asbury Society, Mark birthed the 1995 twenty-fifth anniversary video production, "When God Comes."[1] Mark is the author of books which intersect with the subject of revival, including The Fasting Key[2] *and* No More Spectators,[3] *also available online. He is currently teaching pastor at RiverStone Church in Kennesaw, Georgia. In addition, he has ministered as an evangelist, missionary, and church planter. He and his wife Kathy reside in Marietta, Georgia.*

It was a disappointing chapel service. I was on a ministry team that went to Spring Arbor College in Michigan. We were excited. Unbelievable reports had come from other Asbury College teams and students. Dr. Kinlaw, president of Asbury College during the revival, said one of the marks of true revival is how easily it can be transferred. This was confirmed in colleges and churches everywhere. In the first days of the revival individuals went to Azusa Pacific College in California and Greenville College in Illinois. Revival immediately broke out.

With expectation our team made the long trip and shared in the chapel at Spring Arbor College. To our disappointment absolutely nothing happened. There was no massive move forward by the students. We left thinking we might be the only team coming back without seeing revival spread.

For years I always wondered why God hadn't come like reported in other colleges. I even thought it had something to do with me. Possibly I wasn't prepared spiritually to be a carrier of revival.

Fast forward twenty-four years later. I was the Executive Director of the Francis Asbury Society in Wilmore, Kentucky. Hearing some audio tapes recorded during the Asbury revival, I sensed the Lord directing our ministry to make a video on the revival using these recordings of testimonies and news reports. A gifted Asbury student produced the video, naming the finished product, *When God Comes.*

At the premiere, showing in Hughes Auditorium, Dr. David Gyertson, president of Asbury College at the time, introduced the video for the 25th anniversary of the Revival. To my surprise he started sharing regarding the time our revival team came to Spring Arbor College where he was on staff.

Dr. Gyertson told how the Asbury students shared in chapel with no response but he then stunned me by telling the following. Late that night, after our team was long gone, he said a knock awakened him. He opened the door to find someone reporting that the students were gathering in the chapel and God was moving on them. A revival eventually impacted the Spring Arbor area, lasting for weeks.

That night attending the video premiere, I learned a lesson about revival. The Holy Spirit can use us when two things are offered. In 1970 our little team from Asbury had nothing to offer God but our availability and expectation. For twenty five years I had no clue how the Spirit used that offering to spread revival by means of a disappointing chapel service in Michigan.

[1]*When God Comes: Reliving the Asbury Revival, 1970*, Introduction by Dr. Henry Blackaby (Nashville, TN: Broadman and Holman Publishers, 1995). *[NOTE: This DVD may be purchased through the Asbury University Eagle Outlook, (859) 858-3511, Ext. 2162.]*

[2]Mark Nysewander, *The Fasting Key* (United Kingdom: Sovereign World Ltd, 2015).

[3]Mark Nysewander, *No More Spectators: The 8 Life-Changing Values of Disciple Makers* (United Kingdom: Sovereign World Ltd, 2006).

Heartaches.   In late January, 1970, Wesley L. Duewel and Dr. Eugene Erny, his predecessor in the presidency of the Oriental Mission Society, were in Wilmore for business. Dr. Kinlaw invited them to meet with him and Dean Reynolds. Dr. Duewel wrote, "Both of these men opened their hearts to us, sharing their deep burden for the youth of America, the declining moral standards, the drug problem among youth...." These problems were producing repercussions on campus. "They had a great burden for what should be done. We spent two hours together in discussion and prayer."   One week later to the day revival came. Wesley Duewel, *Revival Fire*, p. 342.

Commencement Exercises, 1970.   Perhaps no alumni association in the history of American education ever listened to such a challenging address on revivalism by a more distinguished scholar. Dr. Kinlaw was heard by a record crowd of over seven hundred alumni gathered in the college cafeteria for the annual alumni banquet. *The Herald*, July 1, 1970, p. 3. AUA.

Gossip.   "Before this revival I could do a lot of things. I could talk about people behind their backs; I could gossip. I used to cut up people just for jokes. I now know that every time I did that it was a strike against Jesus; it hurt Him." Donald E. Demaray, "Revival Witnesses," *The Herald*, 1970. AUA.

Dating.   A piquant brunette who "lost her guy" had told God she hated Him for her loss. But reassured of His love for her, she came to recognize that God must be first in her life. "Will AC Be 41st Campus in Revival?", *Anderson Herald*, Anderson Indiana, Feb. 24, 1970. AUA.

Minister Doesn't Need to Preach.   In 1970 a Baptist pastor announced that he had not preached in five Sundays. His people just got up and witnessed in church and "things happened." AUA.

Tim Philpot - 1970

INTRODUCTION: Tim Philpot is a lifelong resident of Lexington, Kentucky. He was a courtroom attorney for 26 years, concentrating on employment law, family law and civil rights cases. In 1990, Tim was elected to the Kentucky State Senate where he served two terms until 1998. In 1996, he was selected as President of Christian Business Men's Connection International (CBMC), a ministry to business and professional people. Tim retired from CBMC in 2003 to return to his legal career full-time. The Board named him a "Lifetime Ambassador" for CBMC. In January 2004, he was appointed as Judge of the Fayette Circuit Family Court and re-elected to an eight-year term on November 7, 2006. He deals daily with families in crisis.

Looking back, I know the Asbury revival in 1970 has one simple and primary lesson for me. The God of the Bible is to be *experienced*, not just believed.

The 1970 revival was not a time of "decision," meaning a logical and well-thought-out process to decide to follow Christ. Instead, the revival was an illogical, unplanned event, which proved that God goes way beyond our logical ability to figure Him out.

I had an unusual childhood. My dad was an evangelist. I do not recall any decision about going to college. It was a given that I would go to Asbury, the college responsible for my own parents' salvation in the late 1940's.

My dad was on the Board at Asbury in 1970. The Philpot name seemed to give me an advantage at Asbury as I entered as a freshman in the fall of 1969. I was a typical teen. I had played the "Christian" game enough to convince my parents that I was saved and on my way to heaven. But the reality was quite different. I had zero relationship with God. I was a fake, as I told it later.

As I awoke on February 3, 1970, I had already decided to skip chapel that day. That was because I had been to Alabama the night before to watch University of Kentucky play basketball at Auburn. My dad was good friends with Coach Adolph Rupp, and he had arranged an excursion for some of his friends. We arrived back in Lexington in the early morning hours of February 3.

Chapel at 10 a.m. and a test at 11 a.m. was more than I could handle, so I had decided to sleep in slightly and cram for an 11 a.m. exam, ironically in Old Testament.

When I got to class at 11 a.m., not a soul was there. I seriously wondered if Jesus had come and I was the only one left behind at this holy place. I wandered over to Hughes Auditorium. It was full. I found a seat in the back. I watched silently for hours. I recall an older teacher, Mrs. Westerfield, saying to me, "Isn't this wonderful?" I agreed, continuing to fake my Christian experience.

I was mesmerized, as was everyone, by the experience. No one left. The real action was around the altar, but the entire auditorium was full of reverent talk and prayer. It seemed that God had walked into the room. It was not a question of whether to believe. It was more like watching a movie. What would happen next?

The main memory about the first days are certain songs. "There's a Sweet, Sweet Spirit in This Place" was the primary musical memory. It seemed to capture the essence of what was happening.

It was a place of forgiveness. Honesty abounded. People confessed sins publicly. Many were more honest than I wanted to hear.

I have a vivid memory of pastor David Seamands, probably on Sunday [NOTE: sixth day of revival] standing to confess sins himself. Same for a professor named Jim Shephard.

I recall thinking that people at their age and position had surely gotten over "sin" by now. It was shocking. Looking back, I was living in an eighteen year-old's delusion that older "saints" had overcome sin to the point of not needing any more salvation.

On Thursday night at about 10 p.m., the revival had been going about sixty hours. I was sitting in the back and realized it was time for me to do something. By midnight I had the courage to do something, not knowing what that something should be. I stood and walked back to the entrance hall. I stopped a friend and said, "I know you may not believe this, but I am not even a Christian." Her response was to smile and say, "That's no surprise. In fact there are five guys downstairs praying for you right now." She let me know clearly but nicely that I had been fooling no one.

I vaguely recall walking down the right center aisle to kneel and pray. I was immediately surrounded by a dozen or more people. I have zero recollection of who was there. Steve Seamands may have been there.

I specifically recall only two things. One, there was a fellow freshman who, for no good reason, I disliked. He was some sort of eighteen year-old juvenile rival. As I got up from the altar, I kissed him on the cheek and told him I loved him. And second, but related to the first, was my overall sense of Love that had entered the picture for me. I literally loved everyone. Hatred and jealousy and all the negative emotions about other people completely vanished.

I then became quite verbal about this experience. This revival experience was not something I had decided to believe. I had not changed my mind about something religious.

I had experienced something that could be discussed. What analogy fits? I'm not sure, but as I write this I think about some experiences I have had in my life which were "real." I never have any problem telling those stories.

Theories are difficult to explain. But true stories of real experiences are easy to talk about. And the revival was a very true and real story that was easy to tell. So, I went all over America in 1970 telling the story. I continued to experience this revival at other schools, churches, and venues. My own brother and dozens of teenagers at my old high school experienced this same God in a revival that broke out at Tates Creek High School in Lexington. The entire year of 1970 was a time of witnessing to the possibilities of God Himself in our young lives. I learned during that first year of my own salvation that I could trust God to tell me what to say. I never had notes or a script when I spoke of the revival and shared my testimony. God always helped me tell the story in a unique way. God always showed up.

In some ways, 1970 ruined me.

I experienced God up close and personal. I saw what a revival looks like. I saw what church could look like. My own dissatisfaction with church over these many years is partly caused by the fact that I saw what it could be in 1970.

Now, forty-five years later, I have only one disappointment with the revival. It happened in an auditorium with a lot of ecclesiastic symbols and traditions. It was a "church" type revival. And this reinforced for me and many others, I think, the perception that revival is supposed to happen in those kinds of limited places. I still am waiting to see what a revival would look like on Main Street, in the marketplace, in courthouses and business offices.

Does God only show up in holy venues when certain songs are sung and certain words are said?

Hopefully the next revival will answer that question with a resounding "No."

Dennis Kinlaw – 1970

INTRODUCTION: Dr. Kinlaw is a beloved two-term president of Asbury University, and a renowned scholar, teacher, speaker, administrator, writer, warm friend, and more. Someone said that you should never name a building after someone during their lifetime; they might mess up and make you regret it. Even though the Kinlaw Library bears the Kinlaw name, we seem to be safe in this instance.

He appears several places in this anthology, beginning with the revival of 1942. His role as a spokesman and guide in 1970 was crucial. He contributed a short chapter, "The Campus Roots of Revival," to the book One Divine Moment. *There he provides little-known references to colleges like Princeton and Yale, and places American campus revivals in historical context. It's worth the price of the book.*

A format had been developed. It started in that opening chapel. A student would give his witness. He would tell about how God was dealing with him about sin in his life. He'd make his confession. And then he would tell how God had brought forgiveness to him, and restoration. Or how the need of his heart had been met—the spiritual need.

As he would speak, there would be somebody in the audience who would say, "that's like me." And then that person would come under conviction and come forward and kneel at the altar.

So a pattern had been developed of testimony, of sharing. Then after the testimony, prayer, and after the prayer, singing and praise and adoration. And then more witnessing, sharing how God had met human need.

I suppose I had been there about an hour when a young lady came up... and she walked back and knelt beside where I was sitting, and looked up at me and said:

"Dr. Kinlaw, may I talk with you?"

I said, "Why yes."

She said, "I need help.... I am a liar." [NOTE: Dr. Kinlaw broke with emotion as he recounted this episode.]

She said, "I lie so much, I don't even know when I'm lying. I am a liar. Now what do I do?"

Well I sat there for a moment or two, and I had never said this to anybody else, but I looked at her and I said, "Why don't you start back to the last person you remember that you lied to. Confess it to that person, and ask him or her to forgive you."

"Oh," she said, "that would kill me."

I said, "No, it would probably cure you."

Three days later, she came to me radiant, and she said, "Dr. Kinlaw, I'm free!"

I said, "What do you mean, you're free?"

She said, "I just hit my thirty-fourth person and I'm free."

Now that was the kind of thing that was taking place.[1]

[1]Dennis Kinlaw, "A Revival Account," Transcript audio presentation, One Can Happen (blog), Jeff Fenske, https://onecanhappen.wordpress.com/2008/01/30/asbury-revival-1970-dr-kinlaw-i-am-a-liar-now-what-do-i-do/ (accessed 3/31/16).

SNAPSHOTS – Spreading Flame

The Fire Starts Here. Revivals have tended to come to schools where all students were required to attend chapel services. In many schools the students took the initiative in the intercession that prepared the way of the Lord to send revival. Wesley Duewel, *Revival Fire*, p. 320.

A Different Kind of Suitcase College. Asbury is not affiliated with any church. Its students, who come from 40 states and 24 countries, represent 30 separate denominations. One official described the school as theologically "conservative." *Lexington Leader*, KY, May 14, 1970. AUA.

Broken Barriers. The calls for students to come give a report have completely broken down denominational barriers with Lutheran, Baptist, Nazarene, Methodist, Wesleyan Methodist, Free Methodist, Christian and Missionary Alliance, Church of God, Brethren, Mennonite, Church of Christ, Presbyterian, Episcopalian, and independent churches making invitations. J. C. McPheeters, "And the Fire Still Falls," *The Herald*, April 1970. AUA.

Billy Graham Comments. "Some of the greatest revivals in American history have begun at universities. Periodically there have been revivals at such great institutions as Yale, Brown, Dartmouth, Princeton, and many others. It is my prayer that... this spiritual refreshment will sweep from campus to campus and from city to city." J. C. McPheeters, "The Revival Fire Spreads," *The Herald*, April 22, 1970. AUA.

WHAT WOULD PRINCE CASPIAN SAY?

Asbury Revivals Are Interesting but Perplexing

Some readers may be intrigued but relatively unfamiliar with the subject of this anthology, i.e. the God of the Bible may show up in rather unusual ways, as judged by our previous levels of experience. Writing about the Asbury Revival of 1970, *One Divine Moment* editor Robert Coleman captured the scene: "It was as if the campus had been suddenly invaded by another Power. Classes were forgotten. Academic work came to a standstill. In a way awesome to behold, God had taken over the campus."[1]

While such accounts sound exciting, they can also be perplexing, to both unbelievers and believers alike. In many minds, God's greatness often tends to overshadow God's immanence and closeness. Concerning God's greatness, Christians certainly believe God is the Creator of the universe, the Triune One, beyond all knowing, transcendent, eternal, mysterious, holy, unchanging, omnipotent, and all-knowing. Concerning God's immanence, a significant number are slow to believe God is intimately and personally present in creation. This dichotomy is nothing new; early church councils wrestled with it. Examining the life of Christ, their consensus appears in the Nicene Creed. In the incarnate child of Mary, God has indeed come among us.

But How about Today?

At one extreme are secular people who brand as superstition everything outside the bounds of science or limited human experience. In the middle are religious people who believe in God in a generic sense, but whose religion is primarily doctrinal opinions, a system of morality, or the enactment of rituals.

Toward the other side of the spectrum are believers who, in the words of Jesus, are "born from above" (John 3:3). They believe in the Bible and the Holy Spirit. They celebrate God in creation and believe God is present in each new dawn. They recognize God's action through human agents, that of one who plays a beggar's role about our gates, "Meekly to fit My stature to your need."[2] They believe that God places a high premium on agape love, which—if genuine—exerts a powerful attraction (John 13:34-35).

Nevertheless, some believers (maybe many or most from time to time) remain quite skeptical about God appearing in powerful ways on the stage of history—like at Solomon's temple or at Pentecost—to renew and to transform. Especially today. They are reluctant to venture beyond the pages of the New Testament, thinking, "Most of that mysterious and miraculous stuff doesn't happen anymore."

They may ask, "Why would God do such a thing?" It's a good question. Besides the fact God is personal and loves us, another answer is this: when God opens a door to heaven now, it lends support to the truth that God acted similarly in Bible times. "Jesus Christ *is* the same, yesterday, today, and forever" (Hebrews 13:8). World-bound as people tend to become, it's good when God shows up to say, "I'm still here." Succinctly stated, "Give me one divine moment when God acts and I say that moment is far superior to all the human efforts of man throughout the centuries."[3] This issue is especially important in relationship to unbelievers.

Enter C. S. Lewis

We are addressing the question, "How can we know?" Philosophers call this subject epistemology. This book is an anthology of narrative, not philosophy. Nevertheless, it is worthwhile to touch on the question, "How can these things be?" (John 3:9). I propose to do this in light of a popular book entitled *Prince Caspian,* by C.S. Lewis, the brilliant twentieth century Oxford professor and literary giant.

Lewis was an atheist for many years, but he eventually embraced Christianity, partly due to the influence of Oxford colleagues like J.R.R. Tolkien. He was a person with an open mind, one willing to doubt his doubts. He continued to believe that charlatans and superstitions exist, but he began to distinguish between superstition and mystery.

He became convinced that there is "something more out there." In Scripture he found a guide; in *Prince Caspian* he expressed himself on the issue.

A Refresher on Prince Caspian

For anyone who never heard of Caspian, or for someone who needs a refresher, he is a fictional character. Accessible to adults and children alike, *The Chronicles of Narnia* are among Lewis' most popular books. A brief review is in order.

In Lewis's first Narnian book, *The Lion, the Witch and the Wardrobe*, four World War II English school-age children (Peter, Susan, Edmund, and Lucy Pevensie) stumble through a wooden wardrobe into a parallel world called Narnia. They encounter talking animals, fauns, dwarves, and a life or death confrontation with a White Witch under whose spell "It is always winter, but Christmas never comes."

Liberation comes when Aslan—a lion with divine attributes—appears. By dying and rising again, Aslan defeats the White Witch. A golden age dawns until the children (now grown into adulthood) are abruptly drawn back to our world, dressed again in their school clothes. Decades in Narnia were barely a few minutes in England. Having no choice but to resume their former lives, they still have little doubt that Narnia exists. That brings us to book two, *Prince Caspian*.

Centuries pass in Narnia. New evils arise. Young Prince Caspian, another school-age boy, lives under the tyrannical control of his wicked guardian, Miraz. Miraz rules Narnia and keeps Caspian alive only because Mrs. Miraz has no children, and thus no heir.

Caspian's aged nurse tells him stories from the golden age—stories of Aslan, the witch, the young rulers and talking animals. Miraz finds out and disposes of the maid. He scolds Caspian, saying that the stories are fairy tales at best and fools' tales at worst. He forbids Caspian to even mention them.

On a dark night Caspian's wise old tutor, Cornelius, escorts him to the highest point of the castle, apparently for a lesson on astronomy. The tutor has another agenda. Cornelius removes his hood and whispers that the stories are true; he himself is half dwarf. He warns that Caspian's life is in danger. Queen Miraz is about to give birth to a child. Caspian is a rival to the throne: he must escape immediately. A horse and provisions are ready. At this point I refer you to the following abbreviated excerpt.

> "Listen," said the Doctor. "All you have heard about the Old Narnia is true. It is not the land of men. It is the country of Aslan, the country of Walking Trees and Visible Naiads, of Fauns and Satyrs, of Dwarfs and Giants, of the gods and the Centaurs, of Talking Beasts... It is you Telmarines who silenced the beasts and the trees and the fountains, who killed and drove away the Dwarfs and Fauns, and are now trying to cover up the memory of them. The King does not allow them to be spoken of."

> "Oh, I do wish we hadn't," said Caspian. "And I am glad it was all true, even if it is all over."

> "You may well ask why I tell you these things.... I know that you also, Telmarine though you are, love the Old Things."

> "I do, I do," said Caspian. "But how can I help?"

> "You can search through all the nooks and wild places of the land to see if any Fauns or talking Beasts or Dwarfs are perhaps still alive in hiding."

> "Do you think there are any?" asked Caspian eagerly.

> "I don't know—I don't know," said the Doctor with a deep sigh.... I have often despaired; but something always happens to start me hoping again...

> "Then it's true about the Kings and Queens too, and about the White Witch?" said Caspian.

"Certainly it's true," said Cornelius. "Their reign was the Golden Age in Narnia and the land has never forgotten them."[1]

[1] C.S Lewis, *Prince Caspian,* Book 2 in *The Chronicles of Narnia* (Collier Books, Macmillan Publishing Co., New York, 1951), pp. 47-50 selected.

In his flight Caspian soon falls into the company of some native Narnians, and he is caught up in a titanic adventure, Aslan's newest intervention to rescue Narnia and to restore it to its proper condition.

Parallels to the Biblical Narrative

While we may eschew a strict allegorical reading, *Prince Caspian* undoubtedly has parallels to the gospel story. Narnia is in the grip of evil. The benevolent origins and underlying structure of Narnia are largely forgotten due to the influence of those who have, "suppressed the truth in unrighteousness" (Romans 1:18). Yet a remnant remains. Redemption proceeds from sources that are beyond the visible world; "Aslan is on the move." Redemption operates in the world and includes cooperation by faithful Narnians who are ordained and empowered to play a part (Ephesians 2:10), for instance Caspian and the talking creatures. The "good guys" will finally win on an epic scale and in epic fashion.

Isn't this the story of planet earth since the time of the fall (Genesis 3)? Doesn't it continue to this day? Lewis recognized twentieth century intellectual and cultural movements that were veering away from God. He mourned the loss of western culture's classic Christian underpinnings (that is, insofar as western culture is shaped by the gospel), but he held hope that God was ultimately in charge.

Points of Conflict in Today's World

And so the battle lines are perennially drawn. Many opponents resemble Prince Caspian's guardian, Miraz. One such stream arose in the wake of the Enlightenment and extends into post-modernism. These thinkers disallow faith in anything beyond what their eyes can see or science can prove. To them "all those so-called miracles are fairy tales." In this view biblical realities like God, angels, devils, immortal souls, and miracles do not exist. So where do God and spiritual life fit in? They conjure interesting ideas to fill the vacuum.

For instance, there is Sigmund Freud. We may grant his contributions on subjects like psychoanalysis, but when he ventured into philosophy he concluded that God is a psychological creation. He labeled God as a "wish fulfillment," embraced by insecure people who feel a need for something to replace the parents who once took care of them. Similarly, Karl Marx believed faith "God" is a cunning ruse, "the opiate of the people." God is the concoction of oppressive rulers, designed to keep workers from claiming their rightful share of life's labors. They lie by promising deferred gratification in heaven, mockingly calling it "pie in the sky bye and bye." We could quote Jacques Rousseau, Voltaire, Bruno Bauer, Christopher Hitchens, Yuval Harari, and the list goes on.

Despite this chorus of disbelievers, most modern people cannot let go of the feeling there is more to life than—how do we say it?—meets the eye. They sense there are realities beyond what they have seen, at least thus far. They are like Prince Caspian.

The Stories Are True and Two Reasons Why

In summary, were Asbury revivals in-breakings of the living God? Some observers assume naturalistic explanations and look for emotional excess, wish fulfillment, ESP, mass hallucination or groupthink. However, many Asburians believe God did break through. There are at least two reasons to support this position.

One test is practical. We judge a tree by its fruit (Matthew 7). Have people been changed for the good? Troops of Asburians based their lives on the reality of a personal loving God; they sacrificed their lives in love for kingdom service. Good people produce good deeds. By its seventy-fifth year Asbury had placed more missionaries overseas than any other single college in the United States.[4] Graduates such as E. Stanley Jones, Lela McConnell, and Jeannine Brabon (to mention just three) illustrate the positive results.

A second test is rational. Lewis prized logic, personifying it in the old professor in *The Lion, the Witch, and the Wardrobe*. The Pevensie children ask the professor if there could be an invisible world just around the corner. He states that nothing is more probable, muttering to himself, "I wonder what they *do* teach them at these schools?"[5]

Asbury's school motto is "Academic Excellence and Spiritual Vitality." The founders strove to balance the spiritual and the academic. On one hand they determined to start every class with prayer and required chapel services each week, traditions that persist to this day. On the other hand, at the school's inception they designed a challenging classical curriculum with required courses in Latin, Greek, rhetoric, logic, sciences, and more.

Educational standards were often tested by life's hardships. For instance, throughout its history Asbury emphasized study/work options for needy students, including purchase of a farm. But the pursuit of academic excellence endured. In recent years *U.S. News and World Report* consistently ranks Asbury in the top five, including a tie for first place in 2015, out of a pool of approximately three hundred sixty regional colleges in the south.[6] That ranking is not exactly indicative of an intellectually shallow hotbed of religious fanaticism.

Illustrations of the Differing Responses

Modern detractors are cautioned to avoid the plight of the Dwarves (*The Last Battle,* book seven of *The Chronicles of Narnia*), who are so afraid of being "taken in that they cannot be taken out."[7] Again, Susan Pevensie, one of the four original children, does not reappear in *The Last Battle* (this produced some grief in Lewis' readers). Why? Because she has outgrown such childish beliefs, exchanging them for more "grownup" ones, an allusion to spiritual drift and subsequent unbelief (Hebrews 2:1).[8] But most people who have bathed in God's presence are inclined to believe their lives intersect with Someone from another world.

Suffice it to say that reasonable doubt is welcome. It is not enough to say, "You had to be there." People are entitled to ask for reasons to believe. In response, we have appealed to the integrity of the witnesses, tangible results, and Scripture. But it is important to remember that for questions of "what happened?" the science lab has limitations. Science depends on repeatability and a means for controlled testing. Questions of history entail research or a court of law, where human events are weighed. In addition, biblical writers underscore the importance of faith (Hebrews 11:6), not as naiveté, but as openness to mystery and the unknown. Jesus commends the wonder and humility of a child when it comes to the experience of God. In such a vast and beautiful world, this may be the most reasonable stance of all.

A college librarian once confided to me, "I have never had experiences with God. I believe in God but can't recall answers to prayer, a sense of God's presence, or activity from God's side of the relationship. What do you advise?" I replied, "Christians believe that Jesus is risen from the dead. Do not settle for anything less than a Jesus who does stuff." A month later, when we chanced to meet at a bookstore, he joyfully thanked me for helping him. A little puzzled, I asked, "What did I do?" He responded, "Remember you advised me not to settle for anything less than a Jesus who does stuff? Well, He's been doing stuff!"

Final Reasons Why These Matters Are Important

The Savior is risen and moves among us. Something special occurs when a divine call and a commitment to that call combine. Yet even the best intentions wane under normal circumstances. This truth pertains to individual Christians and to the institutions they establish. Numerous organizations and colleges were founded in Jesus' name, but the original purpose is forgotten; today they barely merit the name Christian, at least in the biblical sense of the word.

Joshua's generation witnessed the miracle of the Jordan crossing and conquest of Canaan, but after that generation died, people lost sight of God (Judges 1). Certain factors are needed to keep God central. One of them is a praying remnant who stand in the gap for a new generation. Asbury is fortunate to have had such remnants at several key junctures.

In the final analysis, Asbury's hope is Israel's God and His only begotten Son, the Lord Jesus Christ. When the time is right God periodically removes the veil, steps onto the stage, and attests to His sovereign mystery in the universe. God renews direction and gives assurance to His people. Through them light and hope arise for people still crying in the darkness of a world God loves. Who knows? Even now, Aslan may be "on the move!" May this be our prayer.

Divine visits? Thin places between heaven and earth? Some think these are fairy tales. But I wonder what Prince Caspian would say?

[1]*One Divine Moment*, Robert E. Coleman, ed. (Old Tappan, NJ: Spire Books, Fleming H. Revell Co., 1970), p. 13.

[2]Evelyn Underhill, "Immanence," *The Oxford Book of English Mystical Verse* (Oxford: The Clarendon Press, 1917), http://www.bartleby.com/236/317.html (accessed 4/2/16).

[3]*One Divine Moment*, p. 5.

[4]Henry C. James and Paul Rader, *Halls Aflame: An Account of the Spontaneous Revivals at Asbury College in 1950 and 1958* (Wilmore, KY: Seminary Press, 1966), p.6.

[5]C.S. Lewis, *The Lion, The Witch, and the Wardrobe* (New York: Collier Books, Macmillan Publishing Co., 1950), p. 47.

[6]Edward McKinley, *A Purpose Rare,* pp. 162, 132.

[7]C.S. Lewis, *The Last Battle,* Book 7 in *The Chronicles of Narnia* (New York: Collier Books, Macmillan Publishing Co., 1956), p. 148.

[8]Ibid., p. 135.

Bill Bright – 1970

INTRODUCTION: Bill Bright and Billy Graham were among the foremost Protestant evangelical leaders in the second half of the twentieth century. Bright was founder of Campus Crusade for Christ International. Although he never attended Asbury, he indirectly affected the revival of 1950 and was on the receiving end in 1970.

In 1970, Asbury student Wayne Anthony (1971) traveled to Azusa Pacific College (APC) to give a report about what God was doing. There, as in many other places, the Holy Spirit produced a harvest of recommitments and conversions to Christ. Campus Crusade's worldwide headquarters was located nearby. Bill Bright invited the students to share with his staff. A letter by Larry Shelton, an APC Associate Professor of Religion, describes these events.

Since the report of the Asbury revival was given by Wayne Anthony on February 6 at Azusa Pacific College (APC), the Holy Spirit has continued to move in a very deep way. After the seven-hour chapel service on Friday, the students used the half-time of the basketball game that night to witness to the people from the community who had come to the game. It was a wonderful time. Several hundred students met in the auditorium after the game for another two hour session of witness, praise, and Holy Communion.... Witness teams are regularly going from APC with wonderful results....

Dr. Bill Bright of Campus Crusade for Christ International heard of the revival and called APC to ask for a representative to come to Arrowhead Springs at once to speak to a convention there. Ron Cline, APC Dean of Students, asked me to go, so I immediately drove to San Bernardino and arrived just as the convention of the Southwest Regional Directors of Campus Crusade was being concluded. As I shared with the 100 or so directors about the revival, the Holy Spirit moved beautifully among us. This was the most open and receptive group to which I have ever spoken. There were tears in their eyes and smiles on their faces. This was what they had been praying about for months. A prayer session followed in which they asked the Lord to send His Spirit to their university campuses. I later shared with Dr.

Bright, and as he listened to the reports, this wonderful man of God wiped the tears from his eyes and praised the Lord. He said that this was what he and his wife had begged God to do for years. As I left, he received a call from London, England, and was telling someone there about the revival.[1]

NOTE: There is another story. Years earlier, Asbury was touched by influences emanating from the opposite direction, i.e. Southern California. Campus ministry was springing up across the United States in the wake of World War II. One epicenter for renewal was a Christian ministry center named Forest Home, located in the San Bernardino Mountains of Southern California. The driving force was Henrietta Mears (known as "Teacher"), a staff member at Hollywood Presbyterian Church who had built its Sunday School from a respectable 450 to 4,500 members. It was the talk of the west coast. Bill Bright came to Christ through the ministry of Mears in the spring of 1945.

On a night in June 1947, Mears, Bright, and two other up-and-coming spiritual giants (Louis Evans, Jr. and Richard Halverson, who later became Chaplain of the U.S. Senate) were joined together in earnest prayer at the campground. Something reminiscent of an Asbury revival occurred at Teacher's cabin.

The three of them began to talk and pray. Suddenly they were enveloped in a profound experience. "We were overwhelmed with the presence of God," Bill remembered. "It was one of those things I had never experienced, and I didn't know what to do. I just got on my knees and began to praise the Lord." They were quickly joined by another young man who came to the cabin door and saw Bill and the others on their knees in prayer...Halverson was drawn into the others' experience. "Suddenly he was changed, and he began to praise God with us. It was a dramatic and marvelous experience. We knew the living God had come to take control. And we were so excited we were like intoxicated people." Bill would call it "my first real encounter with the Holy Spirit."

As never before, they sensed the awesome call of God, yet they felt helpless. They wanted to be used of God. What could they do? Where would they begin? "While we were all carried away with the sense of the holy presence of God, our minds were racing with creative ideas." While praying, they saw before them in their minds the nation's teeming college campuses, where an army could be recruited for God....

Later that summer the collegians of Hollywood Presbyterian were to hold their annual summer conference right there at Forest Home. Could they dare to expand that conference to include hundreds of collegians from all over the nation and to share tonight's vision with them? It seemed quite impossible—with less than two months' time—but they determined to set out to accomplish it. Out of that night was birthed what came to be called the "Fellowship of the Burning Heart," a name derived from John Calvin's seal showing a hand offering a heart afire with the inscription: "My heart I give Thee, Lord, eagerly and sincerely."[2]

NOTE: These experiences gave rise to the famous Student Briefing Conferences at Forest Home. The campground became a magnet for thousands of young people drawn to campus ministry. In the summer of 1949, a fledging Billy Graham joined them. Besides his budding ministry of citywide evangelistic campaigns, he had already served as the founding organizer of Youth for Christ and was President of Northeastern University in Minneapolis (at age thirty he was the youngest college president in the United States). Graham delivered the morning lectures at Forest Home and Dr. Orr (see page seventeen on how Orr relates to the 1904 Revival in Wales) delivered the keynote addresses each evening.

Graham was wrestling internally about the inspiration of Scripture. Mears, Orr, and Bright pulled him in one direction, and a young Princeton seminary friend, Chuck Templeton, was pulling him in another. Beginning with a remark by Templeton, here is Billy Graham's see-saw struggle in his own words.

"'Billy, you're fifty years out of date. People no longer accept the Bible as being inspired the way you do. Your faith is too simple.'" ....Alone in my room one evening , I read every verse of Scripture

I could think of that had to do with "thus saith the Lord." I got up and took a walk…. Dropping to my knees there in the woods, I opened the Bible at random on a tree stump in front of me…. The exact wording of my prayer is beyond recall, but it must have echoed my thoughts: "Father, I am going to accept this as Thy Word— by *faith*! I'm going to allow faith to go beyond my intellectual questions and doubts, and I will believe this to be Your inspired word." When I got up from my knees at Forest Home that August night, my eyes stung with tears…Not all my questions were answered, but a major bridge had been crossed. In my heart and mind, I knew a spiritual battle in my soul had been fought and won."[3]

CONCLUSION: The famous Los Angeles Crusade that propelled Graham's ministry into the stratosphere of worldwide ministry began one month later in September, 1949. Also, two of the many colleges affected by the student movement were Wheaton and Asbury. Christian students across the United States heard the exciting news from Southern California. Some set their prayer sails to catch the wind of the Holy Spirit for their own campus (Bob Barefoot among them). More directly, Dr. Edwin Orr, the primary teacher at Forest Home, spoke at both colleges in the years prior to the mega revivals that began the following January at Wheaton, and February at Asbury. Godly workers were planting and faithful intercessors were watering the seed.

The "Wheaton Connection" receives additional attention in relationship to the 1995 Asbury revival.

[1]Shelton Letter, Asbury University Archives, Box 3.

[2]Michael Richardson, *Amazing Faith: The Authorized Biography of Bill Bright* (Colorado Springs, CO: Waterbrook Press, 2000), pp. 36-37.

[3]Billy Graham, *Just As I Am: The Autobiography of Billy Graham* (New York: Harper Collins, 1997), pp. 138-139.

Students Look Back Twenty-Five Years Later – 1970

INTRODUCTION: Phillip Collier, a pastor residing in Tipton, Indiana, completed a Doctor of Ministry degree at Asbury Seminary in April, 1995. He examined the long-term effects of the 1970 Revival on the spiritual lives of student participants. This section contains a few anonymous responses to a random sample questionnaire he sent to 237 students 25 years after the event.[1] What stood out in their minds? Were there lasting results? How did it affect their spiritual lives? A high percentage of the responses were very positive and speak for themselves.

• I felt a tangible change in the atmosphere during that February 3 testimony meeting, sort of like electricity going through the crowd. In the beginning, it was a typical chapel meeting (slow and boring) then it immediately changed. The whole room was "charged" with excitement. It was the greatest outpouring of the Holy Spirit I've ever seen before or since.

• The almost overpowering sense of God's presence during Friday evening. I'll never forget it. The worship and praise that night has remained for 25 years as a model and reminder to me of what worship *can* really be. Through it all, God's love was compellingly manifested.

• I had transferred in for the winter quarter a month before, so I was new to the campus. The beginning was what I remember as much as any other part of it. It seemed a bit unusual when the dean announced he was not going to speak as planned. I was sitting in the balcony [at the] rear of the auditorium. The window behind me was slightly ajar, and sometime during those beginning moments, I heard a sound—like a wind whooshing—soft but not the normal wind blowing through the window. The next seven days were ones of a sweet spirit atmosphere in that auditorium.

• I was in a required chapel service, anxious to get out and go to class. I was a sophomore at Asbury and was not a Christian yet. When the bell rang to go to class, I noticed something unusual was happening and *could feel* it. No one left the auditorium. At first I thought it was great to be missing the next class. Then I paid attention to what was going on, and for the first time in my life I *knew* there was a God and that He was real, *loving* and personal. In the first few hours I just watched, but less than a day later, I had given my heart to Him, prayed with a friend who knew I wasn't a Christian, and I became a Christian and have stayed true to it all my life thereafter. The 1970 revival was *the* most life-changing experience of my life.

• As I recall the Asbury revival, I remember the abiding presence of the Holy Spirit. The Spirit was so evident, it was as if I was inhaling and exhaling the Spirit. It was the precious, sweet, aroma of His presence. Tears flowed from everyone who praised Him. The Lord's might and power were expressed by incredible answers to prayer. Other revivals broke out just by students calling home to relate what was occurring at Asbury. The testimonies of students and those attending sparked revivals all over the U.S. and one revival in Mexico as a student called her home there. The song "There's a Sweet, Sweet Spirit in This Place" encapsulated the aura of Hughes Auditorium. It was as if a magnet was in Hughes, drawing me there. I couldn't leave but for an hour or two at a time; I had to be there day and night. Time was suspended for one week. I tasted heaven.

• I feel honored that God showed Himself in that miraculous way while I was a student at Asbury. Perhaps I experienced enough during that week to never doubt that there is a God who loves me unconditionally. I haven't ever verbalized that thought, but as I'm "forced" to reflect on that time I believe it's true.

• I most recall the student body, faculty, and staff being glued to Hughes Auditorium. No one wanted to leave because the Holy Spirit was moving so powerfully. I recall the students lining up to confess and testify and the ladies trio singing "Fill My Cup." I also recall the places I was privileged to visit, sharing what was happening at Asbury—churches locally, college campuses, and, in the summer, South and Central America.

• What I remember most is that several of the "tough guys" (who had turned rebellious against their parents' faith) came to know Christ in a personal way. They were never the same again. The testimonies touched me as no others did. I also saw people who had held grudges against each other renew their relationships.

• I recall the total spontaneity of it—no preaching, no pleading for people to come to the altar. After hearing so much about being filled with the Spirit, I recall seeking it for myself. That week in 1970 was a turning point in my life. My walk with the Lord came alive.

• I think the first thought that comes to mind is pure unbounded "JOY"! It was such a season of "light and joy." It was as if the very air was easier to breathe! I felt we had been—all of Hughes Auditorium—lifted to a higher plain. The Holy Spirit seemed to particularly settle on that wonderful old auditorium. We were aware of a special giving of His presence all over campus, but it was like Hughes was the "holy of holies" and that God was flowing from there into our lives and then to the world.

• I remember one time, late on the first day or the second day when I found myself sitting behind the altar with my back against the stage just watching all the people praying at the altar and listening to the testimonies—I was laughing with joy. I looked at my watch and realized I had been sitting and laughing for over three hours!

• After initially rejecting the event as just emotionalism, I was compelled to reevaluate my assessment because of the serious deep response to it by my peers and the faculty. My cynicism was overtaken by the reality of all I was seeing.

• A team of us went back to our home churches in West Virginia and shared what had happened in our lives. I've never felt so empowered by God or such an overwhelming spirit of love. At my home church I witnessed people who had been at odds for years forgive and embrace each other as they opened up to "the sweet, sweet spirit" in our midst.

• The genuine change that occurred in the lives of 100 people around me; the confessions of leaders at the school and in the community of the need for change in their lives (people I thought had it all together as Christians); the humility of those people (adults) in leadership to make confessions to the student body. It could have been nothing other than the Holy Spirit moving in that place that caused it.

CONCLUSION: Dr. Stephen Seamands, an Asbury Theological Seminary professor, closely followed the development of this doctoral study and commented on the student responses as seen through the eyes of the writer, Phillip Collier. "Invariably, as they shared their experiences, their eyes lit up and they became more animated indicating the depth of impact the revival had upon their lives. Their memories have several common themes. Most often it was their profound sense of the manifestation of God. It was unmistakably clear to everyone present that God was in the midst of His people. Equally evident was their openness and honesty to God and to one another, as well as a willingness to do whatever was necessary to tear down barriers. Above all, there was a foretaste of heaven where God dwells and reigns in the midst of His people."[2]

[1]Phillip Bruce Collier, "The Significance of the Asbury College Revival of 1970 for Some Aspects of the Spiritual Lives of the Participants," Appendix B. Used by Permission.

[2]*One Divine Moment: The Account of the Asbury Revival of 1970*, 25th Anniversary Edition, orig. 1970 (Wilmore, KY: First Fruits Press, 2013), pp. 101-102.

1977 – Stuart Smith

INTRODUCTION: Stuart might be described as the sheep who tried to get away, but God had other plans. Between the revivals of 1970 and 1992 he came to Christ and was called to leadership on campus.

I was fifteen years of age in February of 1970 when I heard about a chapel service in Hughes Auditorium that was going on continuously. I ventured up to the campus, as my father and mother taught and worked there, just to see just what was really going on. Throughout my life, I had always been in church almost every time the doors were open. This day, however, I was not forced to go but rather was "drawn" to the chapel by what I heard had to be God Himself.

I walked into the back of Hughes Auditorium on the Wednesday of that spontaneous revival week. I immediately sensed the presence of God even though I was not walking with Him in personal fellowship. I knew that the Holy Spirit was speaking to me about my life and I literally held on to an old heat register on the back wall of the chapel. I felt that if I let go of the register I would be doomed to follow God in a way that I had never gone before and to places that I would never want to go. So, I did hold on to the register and also to my selfish and sinful ways; then I bolted out the back doors never to return that week to the place where God was moving in the midst of the campus and community.

I witnessed many individuals who were changed during that week in 1970. I lived in Wilmore and went to the Wilmore United Methodist Church with my family. There I was able to see changes in people that were only explained by the touch of God on their lives during the Asbury revival on the college campus. Even in seeing living testimonies of

God's transforming touch, I continued to live life apart from a personal relationship with God.

I came to saving faith in Christ almost exactly three years from the day when I had walked into Hughes Auditorium and chosen to hold on to those heat registers. I turned my life loose and gave my all to the Lord and committed to living for Him. I also enrolled during that time (1973) as a freshman at Asbury College (now University). During my college years, through the chapel program and Spiritual Emphasis Weeks on campus, I deepened my commitment to love and serve God and all others.

God led me back to Asbury in 1989 to serve as the Dean of Men and then later as the Campus Chaplain. I served in these capacities in the Student Development Department for 20 years. During that time, we were blessed to have other beautiful and powerful movements of God, including 1992, 1995, and 2006. I would have to say that each time of revival was preceded by an intentional prayer effort normally generated from the students themselves. These moves of God came as a chapel message or testimony time "broke through" at the normal conclusion of the service when many individuals stayed and prayed in their seats or (more often) on their knees in front at the altar in Hughes Auditorium.

These "times of revival" always saw students and others seeking more of the Lord for their lives. Many came away from those "times" with a renewed sense of a particular calling of God upon their lives. Relationships with God and with others were restored, and God received praise for coming yet again into our midst and transforming hearts and lives for His glory and for the good of others. My prayer is that the Lord will come again and again and continue to draw His children to Himself so that we might be all that He died for us to be.

DIFFICULTIES AMID REVIVAL

INTRODUCTION: As noted in the introduction to this anthology, the overall tone of the collection is decidedly positive, as it should be. Nevertheless, I composed the following selection based on direct or indirect reflections from people who—though generally a minority— apparently experienced difficulties amid revival. They deserve attention. I hope this dose of sensitivity helps foster healing, resolution or closure where needed.

Why did some students or administrators have mixed thoughts and feelings? Here are a few reflections.

First, everyone is different. Given human diversity, there will always be more than one way to look at an event. The first Fourth of July celebrations were an occasion of celebration for patriots, but one of mourning for loyalists to Great Britain. This reason may end the matter, but often there is much more going on below the surface.

Second, one person wanted to experience what others described, but commented about feeling left out when others expressed deep feelings of contrition, deliverance, reconciliation, or joy. The thought was, "I am not feeling this; is something wrong with me?" In truth, some people may not have been ready. On the other hand, emotion is not necessarily the hallmark of God's visitation. The stories of E. Stanley Jones and Lincoln Stevens are cases in point.

Third, revivals can be messy. Surprised students are newly awakened to God, and the enemy works hard to counteract this. Internally, heresy may creep in. Externally, the apostle Paul and John Wesley faced angry mobs (sometimes stirred up by civil or ecclesiastical authorities). For that matter, so did the Lord Jesus.

Still again, someone may be put off by student exuberance and levels of emotional expression. Some people who favor a high-church Anglican style of worship may believe deep feelings and encounters with God are for the most part best kept to oneself. They are certainly not articulated in corporate worship. Even in less liturgical settings, public declarations of emotion are not the norm. It may be a matter of temperament.

Generally speaking, spontaneous revival in purest form tends to allay such reservations.

Fourth, counseling at the altar or elsewhere can sometimes tend toward over-simplistic diagnosis or prescription. "Just repeat this prayer after me, and God will take care of everything." Often it works, but not always. For instance, someone suffering trauma from childhood sexual abuse may need referral to a professional. No matter how well-intentioned, counselors (faculty as well as students) may be inept or need more training to relate to special needs. Would even the most saintly entries in this anthology make a claim to sainthood? To the contrary, they would all deny it. Even so, this too becomes part of the wonder of the moment. Under the guidance of the Holy Spirit, God uses ordinary people and simple prescriptions to accomplish divine work. Remember that the first disciples boldly testified before the ruling religious council in Jerusalem. Untrained and ignorant men they were, but council members noted that these men "had been with Jesus" (Acts 4:12).

As a positive example, in 1974 I heard Dr. Dennis Kinlaw speak to a sizable number of pre-ministerial students. He related a personal experience from his college years involving a student doing altar work. The student asked him, "You want to get closer to God. So how much time are you spending in morning prayer?" After hearing the answer, the student replied, "Double it." The aspiring spiritual guide inquired again, "How about your daily Bible reading?" Kinlaw gave an answer. The student repeated the same counsel, "Double it." Dr. Kinlaw chuckled as he told the story, but then added, "I discovered great value in reading six consecutive chapters of Scripture at a time; and though I sometimes woke up on my knees in prayer, God blessed it."

On the negative side, about 1971 in the heyday of the Jesus Movement, an intelligent and emotionally sensitive Roman Catholic young man was invited to a rather "raucous" worship service. Late in the service he went forward at an altar call. Why did he go? Perhaps it was because everyone else was doing it, and he was a guest. The pastor who spoke with him was by nature a quiet and unassuming soul;

nevertheless, the guest was rattled. He went home and conversed with his family, who promptly administered a stiff shot of whiskey to settle his nerves. Needless to say, he never returned. Even so, God may have planted seeds that will come to fruition with time and prayer (Romans 8:28).

Fifth, heavenly visitations cannot be programmed. God works in both overt and quiet ways, and speaks in thunder and a whisper. A library administrator kindly expressed her belief that the Holy Spirit perennially operates in a "low hum" at Asbury (and in the world at large, one might add), but breaks forth with more evident manifestation from time to time.

I can testify to memorable occasions when God came close to me on campus. Irish Christian spirituality refers to these as "thin places," times in life and even geographical locations where the apparent barriers between heaven and earth seem to fade away. In Hughes Auditorium, a couple of times after chapel I knelt at the altar as others went on their way. Unnoticed by them, God moved powerfully in my life. Students may recall a walk at sunset, a musical concert, a conversation with a friend, or private prayer times in a dorm room that became "thin places" in their spiritual journey and significant junctures in their walk with God. In the Bible we glimpse the intimate annunciation to Mary in contrast to the public cascades of Pentecost. In each case the Holy Spirit descended, but not in a set pattern. Indeed, the Hebrew word for "spirit" may be translated—along with other connotations—as the untamable wind (see John 3:8). Either way there is cause to celebrate God's coming.

Sixth, one objection is philosophical in nature. If God has come so mightily among Christians, then why are our lives and our world not more transformed? For instance, during his work in India E. Stanley Jones developed a spiritual vision of a world where apartheid, poverty, and war would end, where the lion and the lamb would lie down together, and where swords would be beaten into plowshares. Yet the cause of equality in India was largely championed by a Hindu, Mahatma Gandhi.

Stateside, southern church and college administrations were dragging their feet on integration during the 1950s and 1960s.

Among students, members of the 1969 Collegian editorial staff decried apathetic responses toward racism, intercity poverty, and the course of the war in Viet Nam. If there was a willingness to help the man in the ditch on the road going down from Jerusalem to Jericho, there seemed to be less willingness to address the conditions that made the road such an unsafe place to travel, and why weren't evangelicals doing more to rehabilitate the muggers?

To be fair, the same accusations could be leveled toward Christians in other times and places. We wonder why the end of the slave trade and equality for women took centuries. But come they did. And isn't it true that these advances and many others (education, health care, child labor laws, etc...) came to fruition in countries where Christians gained access to the reins of influence and power? Gandhi claimed that his philosophy of nonviolent resistance was rooted in the Sermon on the Mount, which he studied at Oxford; and it was E. Stanley Jones—the Christian—who championed the rights of politically marginalized untouchables under the proposed new constitution of India. Again, Asbury has stronger connections to the Salvation Army than almost any other college. Is it because the school has the heart of a Salvationist? Revived people will be about the business of their heavenly Father. Is the kingdom long in coming? Yes. Could more be done? Yes. Was nothing done? No.

On a final note, while we acknowledge the tremendous good of spiritual outpourings, we recognize the necessity of diligent follow-up, that is, the spiritual work of grounding newly awakened believers in the faith. John Wesley opined:

> I was more convinced than ever that the preaching like an Apostle, without joining together those that are awakened and training them up in the ways of God, is only begetting children for the murderer. How much preaching has there been for these twenty years all over Pembrokeshire! But no regular societies, no discipline, no order or connection; and the consequence is, that nine in ten of the once-awakened are now faster asleep than ever.[1]

It is possible that one key reason for the positive impact of the 1970 Revival stemmed from the groundwork that was laid when thirty student leaders used *the John Wesley Experiment* (see p. 107) in advance of God's visitation. About two hundred students signed up to participate in the *Experiment* the weekend before the windows of heaven opened. Although it is difficult to say how many students actually followed through amid all the excitement, there was a clear focus on inward and outward spiritual disciples, and a core of seasoned leaders to help model and sustain the work.

This is a New Testament pattern. After Pentecost, Luke writes, "and they devoted themselves continually to the apostles' teaching and fellowship, to the breaking of bread and prayer" (Acts 2:42). In other words, Jesus trained the disciples so that multitudes of newly awakened believers could be nourished and established in the faith.

CONCLUSION: Dr. Joe Brockinton touches on issues of follow-up in his personal reflections, which relate to 1992 and 1995.

---

[1]Mark Gammill, "John Wesley's Clarity in Vision and Strategy: A Necessary Step for the 21st Century Church, Pt. 2," Seedbed (blog), http://seedbed.com/feed/john-wesleys-strategy-necessary-step-church-pt-2/ (accessed 2/1/16).

Gary E. Wright – 1991

INTRODUCTION: Gary's story could bear the title "It Hasn't Stopped Yet." In 1970 he traveled with a witness team to South Meridian Church of God, Anderson, Indiana. Revival swept the church, Anderson University campus, and the city. In Gary's words, "Some say as many as 5000-7000 made commitments to Christ during the 50 days of nightly services that outgrew the Church facilities and moved into the civic auditorium." Here he reports similar happenings 21 years later at another campus, Bethel College, in Mishawaka, IN.

It was 1991. I remember sitting on the front row of Bethel Chapel, which was held in the college cafeteria, waiting to bring the last message of that "Spiritual Emphasis Week." I was only being given 20 minutes to speak. I had a problem. I sensed God was asking me to share about the 1970 Asbury/Anderson revival, including my testimony of being filled with the Holy Spirit. How could I do that in 20 minutes? I prayed, "Lord, you know me, I cannot say 'Hello' in 20 minutes; this seems impossible."

As I sat on that front row next to my dear friends, Bob and Marilyn Ham, I also had an old spiritual sensation inside. It took me back 21 years to the Anderson revival. I felt heaviness in my chest that I remembered feeling as I walked up the steps to the pulpit area on Sunday evening that first day of the Anderson revival. It is hard to explain that feeling. I regard it as spiritual, yet it feels physical. It is the weight of His glory. In Scripture "God's Glory" is defined as that which has weight *[NOTE: The Hebrew word "glory,"* כָּבוֹד, *kavod,[1] is indeed derived from the root "heavy"* כָּבֵד, *kaved]*, as with gold or silver. One feels the physical weight of His presence. His glory contains His Holiness. One can at times sense one's own lack of "holy" and that of others. God seems to have at times allowed me to sense the burden of sin in people's lives. At its strongest it seems at times to take my breath away. I thought to myself as I waited to preach, "God is going to do it again." In the next 20 minutes, He did it again.

People started walking to the altar area of chapel that day before I could finish. Maybe as many as fifty to seventy people knelt and prayed and wept. Soon people were apologizing to each other over one of the microphones. I thought to myself, "This looks and feels real."

It truly has proven to be real revival. I remember sensing the Lord speak to me. He said, "Your work is finished, do not say another word." I saw an empty seat that someone had vacated on the back row of the chapel so, without saying another word, I walked off the pulpit area and sat in that seat. Again, I sensed the Lord speaking to me, "I said, you are done, leave now!" I got up and went to one of the campus leaders and explained that I needed to be on my way. I went to the room where I was staying, packed my bags, and left. I did not return until two years later when we visited the campus.

CONCLUSION: Gary sums up the long-term results. "When the students and faculty left Bethel campus that weekend, the revival went with them! It quickly spread throughout the entire Missionary Church denomination. According to then Missionary Church President Dr. John Moran, the revival had an enduring effect on the denomination that has lasted to this day. Bethel College certainly has never been the same. It has tripled in size as students who seek a deeper relationship with Christ have recognized the spiritual depth on campus. Chapel services continue to be a place where people can experience God."

[1]Eli Lizorkin-Eyzenberg, Jewish Studies Blog by Dr Eli, http://jewishstudies.eteacher-biblical.com/glory-mean-hebrew-insights-dr-eli/ (accessed 3/21/16).

SNAPSHOTS – Points of View
Two Contrasting Views

Yale University, 1827 – Revivals are Good. The revival of 1827 was marked especially "by the conversion of a knot of very wicked young men, whose piety at a subsequent period became equally eminent." The movement spread to New Haven; for every Yale man converted there were nine New Haveners converted. "Its effect upon student morals and order was so great that for a year not a single student was disciplined by the faculty." "Student Revivals Awaken Campuses: Then—Yale's History Marked by Frequent Revivals," *Yale Standard*, Fall 1970. Vol. 2, No. 1. AUA.

Wheaton College, 1970 – These Revivals are Bad. "We must destroy false appeals to authority found in evangelicalism such as equating evangelicalism with Christianity and polluted cliché-concepts with Biblical concepts.... We can only regard the administration's official support of a misdirected revivalism with regret. For such allegiance to old forms, such an easy way out on the part of the administration and of a large portion of the faculty, only means that Wheaton has officially abdicated its proper and imperative role as leader of radical reformation." "Campus Comment: A Reformation Manifesto," *The Wheaton Record*, Wheaton, Illinois, Vol. 92, No. 18, February 20, 1970. AUA.

An Unusual Pattern. In 1970, Dr. Mae Tenny, of Greenville College, Illinois, reported: "The traditional pattern of revival has been broken. There have been no evangelists, no usual altar calls, no pressures except through that Holy Spirit to witness, no formal dismissal.... Seekers come forward quietly. One of the convincing evidences of the work of the Holy Spirit has been the pervading sense of order." AUA.

The Most Popular Subjects of Conversation. Professor Frank Thompson also wrote from Greenville College: "Christ is talked about everywhere. It has become easier for people to love people. There is a new openness among people. There is the unprecedented sight of the most rebellious or uncooperative students finding Christ at altars of prayer. The Bible is becoming a new book as God endorses all the ancient-ever-new promises of salvation and help." AUA.

Student Expression. "The spiritual demonstration there was described as a refreshing form of student expression of no dissent, no protest, no discrimination and one with the complete sanction and blessing of the school's administration. "Miss Sass Tells of Revival at Asbury College." *The Republican,* Meyersdale, Pa, 1970. AUA.

Roy Lauter – 1992

INTRODUCTION: The College was twenty-two years removed from the great revival of 1970. Professor Lauter served as Director of Field Education. He was about to assume a key role in spiritual life on campus. At this time (2016) he is well into his retirement years, but he continues his preaching and missionary work. The following selection is based on personal interviews with Professor Lauter.

As is sometimes the case, the advent of a new administration may give rise to considerable debate about procedures, principles, mission, or institutional goals. So it was in the early 1990s. It was not an easy time for faculty or members of the Board of Trustees. Circumstances came to a head when former president Dr. Dennis Kinlaw officially resigned from his post as Chancellor on February 22nd, 1992. Others were considering a separation. On the student level, top concerns were apparently fairly normal ("the change to semesters, cafeteria food, and parking spaces"),[1] but inside many students were wrestling with deep spiritual and moral issues.

In one respect Professor Lauter reminds one of the prophet Amos in the Hebrew Scriptures. Amos declared that he was neither a prophet, or a son (professional disciple) of a prophet, but a simple man of the land, a shepherd of sheep, and a cultivator of sycamore fig trees (usually cultivated by people of the lowest condition). Likewise, Roy Lauter describes himself as a "country-bred, unsmooth, southern campmeeting preacher." To this day he sees himself as an unlikely candidate to help initiate a campus-wide spiritual renewal. However we may view ourselves, God looks upon the heart.

President Edwin Blue invited him to lead the annual Holiness Conference (Lauter is also an ordained minister). When he declined, the President importuned him to reconsider. After much soul-searching he relented. The services started on Monday, March 30. One may assume that somehow (unseen to the eyes of most) the usual requisite prayer was taking place as the week built to a climax.

The heavens opened on April 3 at the conclusion of the 10 a.m. Friday morning chapel. The student body president stood to speak. He bravely stated that while most of his fellow students perceived him to be a strong person, he was actually a "sham" and desperately needed prayer. After the shock, others followed. Classes were scheduled to resume at 11 a.m. The front of the chapel was filled with young men and women, and although Professor Lauter urged them to go to class, they did not budge from the altar. He felt a nudge, "Leave your post behind the pulpit and go to the floor level; I am in charge here." A large number remained throughout the day and late into the night. At times students would move toward the altar, and then literally fall to their knees partway there, many eventually crawling the rest of the way in abject humility. Truth was coming to the surface… the truth that sets people free. Many returned to spend all day Saturday in Hughes Auditorium, and at various times over the following week.

Insofar as there were few—if any—witness teams traveling outside to other colleges or churches, 1992 was different from the three previous revivals in 1950, 1958, and 1970. Lauter provides some insights. Though he is not one to ascribe personal impressions to the voice of the Holy Spirit, he sensed God saying, "This is not going to be a revival like 1970; it is not intended for the broader world. I am here to cleanse the altar. This is about Myself and My bride." Thus, when someone wanted to video the proceedings, it was vetoed, and similarly with attempts by outsiders (perhaps well-meaning) to steer the gatherings in other directions.

The Board of Trustees was in session the following week. Professor Lauter was invited to give a report. With growing interest, what was supposed to be a short session extended to forty-five minutes. Toward the close he said, "I know that some of you own your own companies, have written books, or are significant contributors. I cannot claim these honors. But I know this. We must recall that from God's point of view, the most important focus at Asbury is to sustain Scriptural holiness." Someone broke the silence with a song as others joined in singing,"Holy, holy, holy, Lord God Almighty...."

Of course, there are individual stories. For instance, a student came to Professor Lauter with a deep sense of contrition, crying and in essence saying, "I have committed a grave indiscretion; I can never atone for it or undo the wrong I did to someone else." Pastor Lauter felt inspired to reply in gentle tones, "Know that you are utterly forgiven and cleansed. Someday you will see this person in heaven, being rocked in the arms of Jesus." The word found its mark and a burdened heart was set free.

In ways known only to God, this revival helped Asbury to remain situated on its foundation. As "Prof" Lauter states, "This move of the Spirit was meant to bring 'Holiness unto the Lord' back to center."

CONCLUSION: There is at least one exception to the "insider" nature of this awakening. Pastor Ron Smith (1977) was beckoned by Asbury students who were members of his church back in New Jersey to join them. He arrived by car on Sunday evening, witnessed it all, and the *following year returned to Wilmore to become a Fellow and then Director of the Francis Asbury Society from 1993-2001.*

[1]Edward McKinley, *A Purpose Rare,* p. 139.

James E. Schroeder – 1992

James E. Schroeder is an attorney in private practice in Hammonton, New Jersey. During his freshman year he became deeply disillusioned and transferred to a state college in New Jersey. That summer he is-sued a skeptical challenge (almost a dare) to a couple of incoming Asbury freshman, and then pretty much forgot about it. He was in for a big surprise.

I entered Asbury College in the fall of 1990. Looking back, I had unrea-sonable expectations of what the Christian college experience would be like. I was a fairly new Christian and was entering a new world 700 miles away from my New Jersey home. What I learned that fall and winter quarter was that things were not as "Christian" as I thought they should be. For this and other reasons I decided that Asbury was not that much different from a public college. So why waste the mon-ey to attend?

Back in New Jersey, a couple of friends were planning to start in the fall of 1991. They pressed me for why I had left and had no interest in going back. I told them that when the Holy Spirit showed up on cam-pus again that I would show up then, too.

I settled into serving on staff at a church, driving a truck, doing odd jobs and studying at the local state college without giving much thought to Asbury other than to inquire about my friends who had enrolled there in the fall.

I came home from work late one Friday evening and my grandmother gave me a message; one of my friends from Asbury left an urgent message for me to call him back. Since they were still using stone age technology in 1992, I had to call him through the pay phone at the end of his hall in Johnson Dormitory. Someone located my friend, who told me that Friday morning chapel had not yet ended. I asked what he meant, and he explained that a testimony chapel was still going on in Hughes and that hundreds of students were there. Professor Roy Lauter had been officially in charge of the morning chapel service. He was still overseeing but more as an observer. I was reminded of my promise.

There were responsibilities to consider, so I could not leave immediately. After confirming on Sunday afternoon that many were still gathered in the presence of God's Holy Spirit in Hughes Auditorium, I preached at my church that night and drove to rendezvous with three other men: Dr. Ron Smith (my pastor), C.J. Caufield (a good friend and now a United Methodist pastor in Mississippi), and Chip Heuera (a missionary friend in Millville, New Jersey). We shared testimonies, sang, and worshiped during the overnight ride to Wilmore. The trip was one of the most enjoyable of dozens I have made along that route.

As dawn was breaking we were marking the last few miles between Lexington and Wilmore. My travel partners dropped me off at the Asbury Seminary Guest House where I had made reservations for the group while they went in search of breakfast, most likely to Pa's Shell Station. As the young woman checked us in, I made an attempt at small talk.

"So, how is the revival going?" I asked. She looked at me, picked up a three-ring binder, and flipped through it. She looked up at me and said, "I am sorry sir, there is no revival scheduled for the seminary this week."

A little confused by her answer I responded, "I'm sorry, I meant at the college. How is the revival at the college going?" She again looked at her binder, flipped a few pages and replied, "I am very sorry but there is no college revival scheduled this week either."

We dropped our bags on the beds in our rooms, washed up, and headed across Lexington Avenue to Hughes Auditorium. As we ascended the steps we could hear the gathered worshippers singing "Holy, Holy, Holy Lord God Almighty. Early in the morning our song shall rise to Thee...."

There was a tangible difference in the air as we opened the doors to the auditorium. The room was filled with worship and worshippers. Students lined the altar and I—still with slight skepticism about the Holy Spirit coming to Asbury after my awful experiences just a year before—slid into a seat near the back of the floor section.

At some point Roy Lauter caught the eye of Ron Smith and asked him to come guide/lead the time around the altar so he could slip home to get fresh clothes and a few moments of rest. I am not sure Professor Lauter had left Hughes in the previous 72 hours. Ron went forward as students continued to take turns giving testimony. There are two things I remember most about the testimonies. First, some of the content was—to put it quite mildly—awful. Second, even though I had spent a year on campus and knew well over half of the student body, I have no recollection who testified to what, just that God was delivering His children from some terrible things in some amazing ways, and it was no one's business who said what.

For the next twelve hours I sat, prayed at the altar, and at one point remember sitting on the floor as there was no seat in the great hall. When I was a student, some of the hour-long chapel sessions dragged on for what felt like days. When I walked down the steps at the end of this time I felt I had been there just moments.

Although I did not return to attend the college, a few years later I studied at Asbury Seminary. The friends who challenged me to return during their freshman year were now college seniors. We enjoyed time together. Even three years later there was a difference in the spiritual temperature as compared to my time on campus just five years prior.

That brief trip to Wilmore continues to have a lasting impact on my life, and I always share my experience with others whenever the opportunity arises.

The Wheaton Connections – 1995

INTRODUCTION: Wheaton College underwent five especially significant spontaneous revivals. The years are 1936, 1943, 1950, 1970, and 1995. The huge URBANA tri-yearly missionary conference grew indirectly out of the lives of students who were spiritually shaped by the Wheaton revival of 1936.[1] Below are reports related to the years 1950, 1970, and 1995. The reader will notice strong parallels and connections between the two colleges, all of it leading up to 1995 when Wheaton directly ignited the Asbury revival of that year.

(1) Year - 1950. Numerous mainstream media and campus news outlets provided coverage. One of the more prominent was an article from Time Magazine, *which was entitled "42 hours of Repentance."[2] Wheaton events began on February seventh, and the Asbury Revival on February 23. Here is a summary of what happened.*

The post-Christmas semester began as usual with traditionally scheduled religious services. On the last evening, President Edman opened the floor for students to come forward to share personal reflections or praise reports. A few testimonies would have been no surprise; but something astonishing happened. Wave after wave of students came to the podium confessing personal sins. It lasted day and night for 42 hours, lines of students waiting for a chance to speak or dedicate themselves to Christ.

Some of the older students had lived through the Second World War (Jim Elliot graduated the year before in 1949). They were a mature group. Students confessed private flaws like feelings of superiority, sexually inappropriate behavior, or something as simple as the habit of saying a prayer of thanksgiving over a meal only to turn around and complain about the food. Faculty joined the chorus. A turning point occurred when Dr. Clarence Hale—a godly and beloved professor— began to confess personal sins. Everyone had to wonder, "Where does that leave me?"

Dean Borgman (1950) was a student worker with campus food service. He went to the meeting when no one came to order any food.

"The revival took me by surprise," Borgman says. "There was no denying the power in Pierce Chapel that first night as lines of students waited their turn to confess. I remember wandering the campus with an overwhelming sense of needing God in a new way. Somehow I ended up in the gym, and threw myself on a wrestling mat with great sobs. I think God was breaking a proud and rebellious spirit in me." Borgman says it was that week of revival and discussions with fellow Bible and theology majors that "produced a sense of wanting to follow Jesus in a radical way, and to change the world through the power of the Spirit." In the years that followed, Borgman went on to become Gordon-Conwell's Chair of Youth Ministries, and in 2014 received a Youth Specialties Lifetime Achievement Award. Borgman's testimony makes one wonder how many more stories of life impact are yet to be heard, as God was simultaneously working in unseen places.[3]

A young baseball player had previously declared baseball (in his yearbook) as his primary interest in life; he gave public testimony that Jesus Christ had now decisively taken center stage.

As word got around, curious outsiders began streaming to campus. President Edman finally called things to an end. Faculty and students were worn out, and much of the sharing was too intimate and sacred for idle ears.

(2) Year - 1970. I have read that students from Asbury spoke at Wheaton, but a larger movement appears to have occurred separately. In any event, Wheaton (like numerous colleges) faced the strains and tensions of this highly turbulent era. Most of the cynicism soon evaporated.

A student at the time, John H. Armstrong 1971, M.A. 1973 remembers what happened during four days of meetings with Rev. Ray Ortlund, Sr. "After four days, there was little evidence of the Spirit doing anything corporately. Suddenly, on Thursday evening, a student asked President Hudson T. Armerding 1941 if he could share his story." Others unexpectedly came to speak, and "within less than an hour, many wanted to speak. Conversions began to happen, and people poured into the chapel." Thanks to a live broadcast on WETN *[Note: Armstrong reports],*

...many began to come from their dorms and from the city. A large crowd had gathered by 10 PM, and the meeting went on through the night. The entire weekend, a spirit of joy and transformation pervaded the campus. Cynicism was altered. Churches were touched. Dr. Armerding asked me to speak in a number of places, and I found high school students receptive and churches listening with joy. I spoke at Trinity Evangelical Divinity School and other schools as well. The fame of what God did at Wheaton lit a flame elsewhere, far beyond the college community.

The son of the guest speaker, Dr. Raymond C. Ortlund, Jr. 1971, notes the ongoing effects of the revival.

The Holy Spirit, I believe, gave us the courage to make wrong things right and get a fresh start together.... The 1970 revival decisively and wonderfully transformed the general atmosphere on campus for the remainder of my time there.... I can never look at anyone, myself or others, and conclude that that person is beyond the reach of God's grace. With Jonathan Edwards, I believe that revival is God's standard strategy for advancing his cause with dramatic acceleration. To have witnessed it personally is thrilling—I want to see the Lord do that again![4]

(3) Year - 1995. NOTE: Interestingly, the Wheaton revival that spilled over to Asbury was in turn sparked by students from Howard Payne University in Brownwood, Texas, who shared testimonies of God's work there. Wheaton's revival lasted several days. Here are a couple of poignant descriptions.

A graduate school student in spring 1995, Holly Gilbreath Bell M.A. 1995, expressed God's tangible nearness during the prayer meetings. "It was just so strong and so thick, like the Spirit was so thick. I never, ever experienced anything like that in my whole life," she says.

Erik Thoennes M.A. 1994, M.A. 1995 remembers one particular example of forgiveness and reconciliation.

A young man confessed racist attitudes, especially toward the Asian students on campus. With tears, he confessed that he had especially denigrated Asian students during his time at Wheaton. He earnestly asked for forgiveness. I was standing in the back of Pierce Chapel with several Korean students. They were also part of the Korean fellowship group on campus. They listened to the confession with intense seriousness. When the student finished, he broke down in tears, and sat down in the front row—face in his hands.

By this time the aisles had become filled with students praying for themselves and each other, some of them prostrate—others weeping and laying hands on one another and praying for the power of the gospel to more deeply invade hearts. The second this young man sat down, the brothers who were standing next to me all immediately started climbing over people and pews to reach this broken man. Once they did, they embraced him, cried with him, expressed forgiveness, and prayed for him. It was a powerful display of the reconciling power of the gospel.[5]

NOTE: Wheaton President, Dr. Duane Litfin, learned indirectly about the move of God. (It started during a regular Sunday evening World Christian Fellowship meeting on campus.) He wanted to support what he sensed was an answer to his prayers, but he was afraid his presence might somehow interrupt or dampen the services. He knew the services enjoyed excellent leadership, so he stayed away at first. Once there, he rejoiced in the testimonies, but felt overwhelmed by the level of need. Here are his reflections about his personal dilemma... and how God resolved it.

I was sitting near the end of a pew. Suddenly a young man appeared and knelt beside me.... This second-year student somewhat nervously whispered to me that he sensed the Spirit of God prompting him to come over and offer to pray for me if I had any needs. And then, having been obedient, but understandably desirous of getting the ordeal of confronting the president over with, he started to get up and said, "I'll be right over here if you need me."

I put my hand on his shoulder and asked him to stay. I told him briefly of the sense of burden I was experiencing and asked him to pray.... Starting somewhat hesitatingly, he prayed, "Lord, I don't even know how to pray for Dr. Litfin." But very quickly he moved off into what I sensed was a very powerful prayer, in the midst of which he said, "And Lord, I ask that you would enable Dr. Litfin to see each of these confessions, not as a burden, but as a gift from you." And immediately his prayer was answered. I was flooded by a sense of peace.... I could not control what was happening and should not try. The messiness of it was inevitable—such things will never be neat and tidy. But God was in it and I was to keep my focus on him, just like everyone else.... in the end He would meet the needs of these students in His own way.[6]

CONCLUSION: In 1995, Wheaton students received many requests from other colleges to come and share their story. Asbury was among them.

[1]Rich McLaughlin, "The Essence of Revival," Wheaton College, Media Center, http://www.wheaton.edu/Media-Center/Wheaton-Magazine/Spring-2015/Feature-Articles/Wheaton-College-The-Essence-of-Revival (accessed 4/2/16). Content by Permission of Wheaton College Department of Archives.

[2]"Wheaton College Revival," *Time*, February 22, 1950.

[3]Rich McLaughlin, "The Essence of Revival."

[4]Ibid.

[5]Ibid.

[6]Duane Litfin, "Afterword," *Accounts of a Campus Revival: Wheaton College, 1995*, Timothy Beougher and Lyle Dorsett, eds. (Wheaton, IL: Harold Shaw Publishers, 1995), p. 155. Used by permission of Wipf and Stock Publishers.

SNAPSHOTS - Wheaton
Deeper Issues Amid Campus Spiritual Renewal

A Psychiatrist's Point of View. NOTE: *Dr. Philip B. Marquart was a psychiatrist and professor of psychology at Wheaton from 1945-58. This is from a letter dated March 6, 1950.*

Now here are some of the astounding psychological facts.... Several dozen cases of emotional problems melted away in revival. I lost all my student counseling interviews. One by one they came around and declared that they were cured.... Then I began to get an avalanche of new patients. Most of them were under conviction—and in conviction it is possible to get every kind of mental abnormality, as long as they resist. One student who had scoffed at the revival became beset with a serious phobia, a fear that he might be catching epilepsy.... Secular methods were of no avail. I finally led him to confess to the Lord. Here he resisted. He had scorned the revival in the first place because he was against confession. As soon as he confessed, his phobia left him. Mary Dorsett, "Wheaton's Past Revival," *Accounts of a Campus Revival: Wheaton College, 1995*, pp. 67-68.

Questions of Genuineness. Long before revival came to Wheaton in March 1995, I had asked a member of Wheaton College's Class of 1950 how she knew there had been a revival that year. "How could you miss it?" she emphatically responded. "For those who were present, it was indeed impossible to miss. Even those who came to the meetings to ask questions or scoff were usually convinced that something genuine and profound was happening to people's souls." Lyle Dorsett, "Wheaton Revival of 1995: A Chronicle and Assessment," ibid., pp. 83-44.

The Depth of Pain, Dr. Ben P., Chaplain, an Upper Midwestern College, 1995. NOTE: *This church-related college underwent a revival after Wheaton students spoke there in April 9, 1995.*

Confession included gossip, spiritual laziness, cheating, sexual immorality, rape, abortion, eating disorders, alcohol abuse, broken relationships, and more. After each person confessed, he or she would be mobbed by peers who encouraged them and prayed for them....

The Holy Spirit was present. Commenting on his own pain at hearing his students' struggles, Chaplain Ben wrote, "It seemed, at times, that a whole generation has been sacrificed to Moloch. Good Friday, which came later in the week, was never so meaningful. To think that Christ bore all that." Chaplain Ben also said that the campus revival demonstrated that students are hungry for "an experience of the church and confession and forgiveness that goes deeper than the cerebral cortex. They don't want a faith that goes against reason, they want a faith that goes further. They understand with Pascal that 'the heart has reasons which reason does not know.'" Matt Yarrington, "The Spreading Blaze," Ibid., p. 155.

Joe Brockinton – 1992 and 1995

INTRODUCTION: Dr. Joe Brockinton was Dean of Students for several years, including 1992 and 1995, when spontaneous revivals occurred along the pattern of previous ones. Society at that time was changing as people "let it all hang out." For example, in 1993 ninety million viewers watched Oprah Winfrey interview Michael Jackson sharing painful details about his personal life. On the positive side, a plethora of self-help groups like Alcoholics Anonymous and Weight Watchers had harnessed the trend for healthy purposes. Dr. Phil, on the other hand, would soon take it to the absurd.

Even so, widespread vulnerability and transparency rarely occurred in a context—especially a college context—with a legacy of holiness, prayer, personal repentance, proper amends, and transformation by God in the light of biblical truth... all toward the goal of mission.

Dr. Brockinton points out especially how campus leaders applied the lessons they learned in 1992 to better preserve spiritual fruit in 1995.

To set the stage for my reflection on the revival that occurred at Asbury College in 1995, I must start with a brief reference to a revival that occurred in the spring of 1992. During the annual Holiness Conference, Professor Roy Lauter challenged students with the message of holiness. At the Friday morning chapel, the student body president shared briefly prior to the message about his own personal struggle to overcome the bondage of sin. It was a bold statement from a student who was looked up to as a model of what a Jesus follower would look like. As "Prof" opened the Word to 2 Samuel 13, he spoke on the theme "But Amnon had a friend, Jonadab" as he addressed sexual purity. At the close of the service, students flooded the altar as the Holy Spirit convicted students of sins. For the next four days, students stayed in Hughes Auditorium and shared testimonies of confession, deliverance and victory.

While this revival certainly changed lives, there were a number of concerns. First, some testimonies left students feeling very vulnerable and unsupported. Second, a number of students returned to school in the fall bitter that their experience had faded, leading them to believe that somehow the experience was invalid. Third, a number of faculty and staff realized that we had not been prepared for this kind of confessional revival and had not followed up with students in providing discipleship groups which would nurture the experience and create a pathway to growth. We determined that should the Holy Spirit move in this way again we would be ready to provide the support needed for growth.

The Holiness Conference in April of 1995 presented such an opportunity when a group of students from Wheaton College (IL) came to campus on Monday night, April 3, and shared about a spontaneous confessional revival that occurred at Wheaton when two students from Howard Payne University (TX) shared how God had moved on their campus. The focus of their witness was that when the Holy Spirit moved, men and women stood and confessed their sins and asked forgiveness. In 1970, Asbury students traveled across the country, including to Wheaton College, sharing about that "One Divine Moment" and saw that revival duplicated in every venue where they shared. Now the Wheaton students were sharing their story, and revival came to the Asbury student body.

The meeting had begun at 7 p.m. and after a brief altar call, students went to the microphone and began to confess sins in order to be healed (or made whole) as proclaimed in James 5:16. Many students declared that God had forgiven them but they felt the need to confess publicly so that they could be cleansed, affirming Wesley's proclamation that Jesus breaks the power of canceled sin. The range of sins confessed included ungratefulness, sexual immorality, pornography, abortion, eating disorders, negative attitudes, and sexual abuse. The testimonies continued throughout the night, and the meeting ended Tuesday morning at 6 a.m.

Following the Tuesday night Holiness Conference session, the confessions continued as students responded to the promptings of the Holy Spirit until about 1:30 AM. This pattern continued on Wednesday night. As I interacted with students it was clear that we needed to implement the action steps we had discussed in 1992. In my journal on April 4, I acknowledged the vast responsibility and wrote, "Lord, help us."

One of the obvious revelations during this revival was the power of two of Satan's most subtle lies. The first is that "you are the only one with this sin" and the second is that "if you confess your sin, you will be rejected by the faith community." The reality was just the opposite. Many students confessed similar sins and found strength in being able to be held accountable by another brother or sister who clearly understood the power that unconfessed sin can have in one's life. Instead of being rejected by the faith community, they were accepted and embraced by the love that characterizes a Christ-centered community.

A staff colleague came to me and confessed sexual struggles as we prayed together and banded together as brothers to hold one another accountable. A freshman couple came to me after chapel and asked me to hold them accountable in their dating relationship as they desired to grow as a man of God and woman of God. Personally, the Holy Spirit convicted me of broken relationships that I needed to repair, and I went to at least two individuals and confessed my bad attitude, asked for and received their forgiveness. This time we were ready to implement some action steps and a number of students responded to our challenge to make this event a beginning of intentional spiritual growth, not just a mountain-top experience that fades over time. To that end, we communicated some lessons we believed would facilitate long-term sustainable growth. Here are some of the messages we presented to students.

This type of public confessional revival is not the norm. In a healthy Christian community confession is generally limited to the circle who either have been affected by the sin or are committed to holding one accountable. If we regularly confess our sins to God and to each other, there will seldom be a need for public confession.

- Becoming a disciple is a process that works best when done in community. The challenge to get into the Word of God and to develop spiritual disciplines is fostered when other believers spur one another to grow in faith and in the works that follow.

- Spiritual growth requires intentionality. The growth curve will be proportionate to the commitment one has to the process. In addition to being involved in a small group of growing disciples, we are called to be the hands and feet of Jesus as we serve others whom God puts in our path. We encouraged students to become actively involved in a local church.

- Many of the faculty and staff volunteered to mentor students who desired to have a Paul and Timothy relationship. These relationships cultivated and nurtured the seeds that were planted in the confessional revival.

The Holy Spirit has chosen to visit Asbury College many times during the history of the institution. Since its completion in 1929, Hughes Auditorium has usually been the place where God's Spirit moves. In almost every situation, it has been the students who have responded to the movement of the Spirit, which has then filtered down to faculty and staff. Every time He comes, lives are changed.

CONCLUSION: Believers in the Wesleyan tradition are keenly interested in the follow-up of newly awakened or recommitted believers (whether by means of classic catechesis, Methodist-style "class meetings," or principles and tools honed by the Navigators). John Wesley's admonition is so important that it bears repetition.

I was more convinced than ever that the preaching like an Apostle, without joining together those that are awakened and training them up in the ways of God, is only begetting children for the murderer. How much preaching has there been for these twenty years all over Pembrokeshire! But no regular societies, no discipline, no order or connection; and the consequence is, that nine in ten of the once-awakened are now faster asleep than ever.[1]

Dr. Brockinton's reflections underscore the value and necessity of preparing for spiritual harvest. But the other side of revival is preservation of the fruit. Without it the work is incomplete. The types of activities practiced in connection with the John Wesley Experiment need to become lifelong habits. They include: (1) a focus on Christ as the center, (2) a commitment to obedience, (3) use of Scripture with a view to application, (4) prayer, (5) small group participation that is characterized by transparent love, encouragement, and a measure of mutual accountability that fosters commitment but not legalism, and (6) witness. If prayer helps to plow the ground and bring rain, then "Life2Life" (that is, one-on-one discipleship or mentoring) and small groups help maximize the harvest thirty, sixty, and even one hundred fold.

[1]Mark Gammill, "John Wesley's Clarity in Vision and Strategy: A Necessary Step for the 21st Century Church, Pt. 2," Seedbed (blog), ibid.

David Gyertson –1995

INTRODUCTION: Dr. Gyertson served as President of Asbury College from 1993 to 2000. Under his leadership the school experienced remarkable advances. Communications, the equine program, enrollment growth, and outside recognitions are among them. Like the founding fathers, he pursued a vision of balanced scholarship and spirituality, and is credited with the school's current motto, "Academic Excellence and Spiritual Vitality." Dr. Gyertson's personal reflections describe how he was touched by God's hand of grace during this lesser-known but important awakening, which began in chapel in February 1995. He also shares how his first experience with an Asbury revival occurred in 1970 when he was Dean of Students at Spring Arbor College, Michigan. At this time of writing, Dr. Gyertson is Dean of the Beeson International Center for Biblical Preaching and Church Leadership at Asbury Theological Seminary.

I am thankful for this opportunity to reflect on God's gracious work of spiritual renewal that has taken place across the history of Asbury University. I know of very few institutions where His Holy Spirit's interventions have been so persistent and consistent. Before speaking to how He touched our campus during my season of leadership at the college, let me set a personal context.

In 1970, I was the newly appointed Dean of Students at Spring Arbor College in Michigan when two students from Asbury came and shared in chapel. It had been a difficult year for the campus with some serious discipline problems. I was awakened at home late that Friday evening by an employee who had come by the house to tell me something was happening on campus. Fearing the worst, I arrived to find the lights on in the college church and perhaps 100 or more students praying, having been awakened by the Holy Spirit and compelled to go to the sanctuary to repent, seeking God, and interceding for the school. For much of the next few weeks, classes and student life were interrupted with times of worship, praise, repentance, and reconciliation. Several students were miraculously and permanently changed. A number were called into Christian work and are serving God's purposes faithfully to this day. Many others stepped into their careers and callings imprinted by what they had experienced in our "One Divine Moment" at Spring Arbor.

That experience laid a foundation for my coming to Asbury Seminary in the 1980s, the decision to send our daughter to Asbury College in the 1990s, and then later to accept the call to come as the President. When I accepted the appointment in 1993, it was during one of the more difficult periods in the history of Asbury. It became clear that we needed the Holy Spirit to bring new unity that would only come from a common commitment to our historic mission and a Holy Spirit calling to reconciliation, repentance, and forgiveness.

In regard to unifying around the core mission, I believe the Lord led me to a restatement of the college's historic motto of *Eruditio Et Religio*—erudition and religion. I experienced two main divisions on campus. Fearing that irrationality, emotion, and perceived irrelevance of the holiness message and experience would compromise the academic quality of the school, there were those who felt that academic excellence anchored to the liberal arts should be the priority. The institution was facing some re-accreditation issues requiring significant efforts in upgrading academic resources—not the least of which was a new library. Others believed that the mission of Asbury was anchored to a vital spiritual experience which they felt was eroding because of an overemphasis on academics. I believed my calling was to show how both were at the heart of the institution's founding and must be mutually informed, infused, and interdependent if we were to be faithful to God's vision through John Wesley Hughes, Henry Clay Morrison, Dennis Kinlaw, and so many others across the decades.

Using a simple metaphor, I concluded that the Christ-centered educational "cart" that Hughes constructed to carry his vision forward required that both "tires" be balanced and equally inflated to accomplish God's rare purpose for this institution. "Academic excellence and spiritual vitality" was my attempt to recover that conviction. Some may have wanted "spiritual vitality" to be stated first, but my decision was to respect the order of the wording formulated by the historic *Eruditio Et Religio* motto. I believed then, and still do, that the truly enlightened understand that spiritual vitality is the way to ultimate Truth and that the spiritually mature, as Paul exhorted Timothy (2 Timothy 2:15), seek understanding that enlightens, fuels, guides and guards their spiritual formation. From time to time, one or the other of the "tires" needs special attention. Whether it is a season of enhanced erudition or of focused spiritual renewal, the genius of the Asbury experience is the recognition that both must be at operating at optimum levels if God's purposes are to be accomplished.

For me, two Divine Moments punctuated the confirmation of this calling to anchor our future to academic excellence and spiritual vitality. The first was the miraculous funding of the library in order to address the potential threat to our regional accreditation. I believe this was the largest fund-raising challenge undertaken in that time. I recommended, and the Board agreed, to name the main section of the Library after Dr. and Mrs. Dennis Kinlaw. I felt this would send a clear message that, as was evident in their life and legacy together, academic excellence and spiritual vitality can coexist in a mutually enlivened environment. The decision to construct the library on front campus next to Hughes Auditorium was intended to show these two distinctives standing side-by-side illustrating Dr. Hughes's dream for future generations.

The second confirmation was a spontaneous revival among the students in February of 1995 that confirmed God was not done at Asbury and that, as it has been throughout our history, the mission would be accomplished "not by might, nor by power but by my Spirit says the Lord" (Zechariah 4:6). While controversy developed over some manifestations being attributed to the Holy Spirit, the major evidences that God was once more visiting the college included deep conviction about living a holy life, repentance, reconciliation, and genuine worship. Along with many of our faculty and staff as well as students, I frequently found myself at the Hughes Auditorium altar those days experiencing the deeper work of the Holy Spirit being done in all of us. While not as dramatic or as sustained as the 1970 movement, there was little doubt that God was visiting a new generation of Asburians with both cleansing and calling as the fruit of His work.

One of the most powerful evidences of reconciliation in the context of this season of renewal came when the President of Asbury Seminary, Dr. Maxie Dunnam, and I concluded that there also was a need for institutional reconciliation. The Spirit led us to seek permission to close Lexington Avenue for a few hours, place a communion table in the middle of the street between our two campuses, and call our respective communities to repent for past and present animosity. Using Nehemiah's confession that "both I and my fathers have sinned" (Nehemiah 1:6), Maxie and I publicly asked forgiveness of each other, washed one another's feet, and then called our campuses, which we had closed for those hours, to come together at the Table of the Lord. Now, having recently returned to the Asbury communities,

I have been told several times that this was a major turning point in the relationship between the two institutions.

It was ministering and being ministered to at the Hughes altar, and so many other places on campus, during this season that my own spirit was assured that God was working and that I should keep going until it was clear that my leadership chapter had concluded.

Looking back on our history, I believe that we must reinforce this missional distinctive of our beloved Asbury and keep faith with John Wesley Hughes and those who sacrificed to make his high calling a reality. While the focus in this publication is on the revivals, I believe we must remember that these did not take place independent of the Eruditio purposes that drove Dr. Hughes to his bold enterprise. There has been a false dichotomy, perpetuated across church history, that the life of the enlightened mind and the surrendered, sanctified heart cannot coexist—that one must be emphasized above the other. The genius of the Asbury mission, and the hope for its continued contribution to our Lord's Kingdom, is openness to God's sovereign interventions that ensure that both are addressed with dedication, sacrifice, courage, and humility.

I close with one final thought about the fruit of redeemed minds and transformed hearts. Out of each of these revivals came, for so many, their call to service. The real evidence of renewed minds and sanctified hearts is hands willing to do His work wherever, whenever, and whatever the cost. Enlightenment and revival are means and not ends. Those who out of obedience surrender their minds to revealed Truth and then "tarry in Jerusalem until they are empowered from on high" (Luke 24:49) are compelled to go into all the world with the Good News (Matthew 28:19). Such I believe was John Wesley Hughes's obsession. This I believe is Asbury's legacy.

My generation now looks to the next to embrace the distinctive calling of Asbury to seek both the renewed mind and the holy heart. I am thankful for the faithfulness to this mission that those who followed me have courageously demonstrated—Dr. Paul Rader, Dr. William Crothers, and now Dr. Sandra Gray. All of us who exercised the privilege of leadership owe a great debt to faithful Board members, faculty, staff, alumni and constituents who stood with us in this sacred mission. May those who come behind us know that we were faithful to those who came before us in this great challenge of discipling Asburians enlightened by renewed minds and empowered by sanctified hearts—all for the goal of glorifying God by equipping holy hands to serve our needy world.

SNAPSHOTS - Music and More

Musical Guidelines for Radio Programming. In October 1928, in response to a suggestion from Newton King, a local pastor, Louisville radio station WHAS and Asbury College agreed to present a daily devotional program from campus. The Board recognized the possibility of "good and evil in radio," but the national crisis demanded a spiritual solution. It was the Asbury mission to provide it. The Board laid down stringent rules for the programs, which began in November. They did not want jazzy or classical material. The music was to consist of "the old standard hymns and the modern holiness hymns." Sermons were to be typed in advance and reviewed by a special committee. ATL

Some Popular Revival Songs

    a) 1950 - To God Be the Glory
    b) 1970 - There's a Sweet, Sweet Spirit in this Place; To God Be the Glory
    c) 1992 - I Exalt Thee; There Is a Balm in Gilead

- 1910. First officially recognized campus band (comprised of seven mandolins and two guitars).

- 1933. The first Class Hymn—"Must Jesus Bear the Cross Alone?"

- Revival musicians were givers of gifts more often heard than seen. One was Lynn Smith, 1970.

- May 1970, the first Ichthus Christian rock festival was held in Wilmore. The festival closed in 2012.

- There is a 33-rpm record of music from the 1970 revival (AU archives has a copy).

- Revived Christians sing a new song—Charles Wesley is the second most prolific hymn writer of all time and is credited with writing over 6,000 songs. Fanny Crosby, another Methodist in the holiness tradition, is the most prolific composer of hymns, with over 8,000 to her credit.

Fatigue Factor?   A doctoral dissertation related to Wheaton College states that the revival of 1995 was the first large-scale revival (the others occurred in 1936, 1943, 1950, 1970) when classes were not officially suspended. An observer noted that an intense fatigue factor developed among the students.

EMBARRASSED BY THE SUPERNATURAL?
Roger E. Olson

INTRODUCTION: The following series of excerpts are pertinent to the subject of God's transcendence, imminence, and the miraculous. They are derived from an article[1] by Dr. Roger E. Olson, professor of Christian Theology and Ethics at the George W. Truett Theological Seminary at Baylor University, and were followed by a clarifying interview with Dr.

Olson. He is the author of numerous books, including: 20th Century Theology *(co-authored with the late Stanley J. Grenz);* The Story of Christian Theology; *and* The Journey of Modern Theology. *He is the current editor for the upcoming* Handbook of Denominations in the United States, 14th Edition, *Abingdon Press.*

Editor: *People say they believe in but act as though they do not in believe in miracles. The claim may be truer than we realize. Do you agree?*

Olson: I teach modern theology in an evangelical seminary.... My students routinely react negatively to the secularism of much modern theology and much of modern theology's accommodation to Enlightenment rationalism and naturalism. However, they are also routinely bemused by my claim that, by-and-large, American evangelical Christianity, including most Baptists, has also accommodated to modernity's rationalism and naturalism.

How so? they rightly ask. My foremost claim is that most contemporary American evangelical Christians only pay lip service to the supernatural whereas the Bible is saturated with it. To a very large extent we American evangelicals... have absorbed the worldview of modernity by relegating the supernatural, miracles, scientifically unexplainable interventions of God, to the past ("Bible times") and elsewhere ("the mission fields").

Editor: *What is your opinion of C.S. Lewis's definition of a miracle?*

Olson: A "miracle," Lewis rightly explained, is not a "violation of a law of nature" as if God had to "break into" and disrupt an autonomous natural system. That is a deist view of God and nature, not a Christian one.

Editor: *Why do so many Christians in the West discount the miraculous and supernatural?*

Olson: I suspect our contemporary evangelical avoidance of the supernatural in the physical realm of reality has little to do with intellectual questions and issues. I suspect it has more to do with culture, with wanting our religion to be respectable.... The abuses of the supernatural seen on cable television may cause us to reject the supernatural entirely. But, as the old saying goes, the cure for abuse is not disuse but proper use. We have thrown the baby out with the bathwater.

Editor: *What can you say about the perspective of Christian students studying in the U.S. who come from Asia, Africa, and Latin America?*

Olson: When they open up, they often say that they are shocked by American Christianity—including evangelical Christianity—because of its individualism, consumerism, and lack of belief in the "spiritual world," by which they mean the supernatural.

[1]Roger Olson, "Embarrassed by the Supernatural," *Good News Magazine*, July/August, 2015, pp. 34-37.

SNAPSHOT
Different Kinds of Trouble

Dr. Robert E. Coleman touches on the fact that both spiritual warfare and natural human hindrances (external and internal) often appear when renewal occurs. The church at Ephesus is perhaps the best biblical case in point, as described in Acts 19 and Ephesians 6:10-20. At Ephesus, spiritual, commercial, and societal forces coalesced, seeking to destroy God's work... to no avail.

Opposition will be most pronounced from those who do not want a spiritual dimension of life. Some will be repelled by the personal moral changes called for by the revival; others resent its social implications. Whenever practical holiness is manifest, antagonism can be expected from the carnal mind, which is against God. Such antagonism may even come from within the religious community.

On the other hand, we must remember that there are human failings even among those who experience revival. Regrettable as it is, spiritual renewal does not make one any less a finite man or woman. Ignorance, emotional instability, personality quirks, and all the other traits of our fallen humanity are still very much in evidence.

Though the revival is not responsible for these shortcomings, it has to bear their reproach.   Robert E. Coleman, "What is Revival?", *Accounts of a Campus Revival: Wheaton College*, pp. 16-17.

Awareness in the Twenty-First Century

Like other Christian institutions of higher learning, the University displays heightened awareness and concern for wider global issues such as the environment, income disparities, human trafficking, and injustice. The sustainable agriculture "Mission Farm" program is one instance where a broadening perspective takes tangible form.

https://www.asbury.edu/academics/departments/christian-studies-phi-losophy/news/2011-09-new-project-connects-ministry-scienc [sic]

Travis Spann – 2006

INTRODUCTION: Travis is connected to two well-known Asbury families, those of Dr. Harold Spann and Dr. Robert Neff. Travis and Charis Spann married in September 2007. Their daughter Zion was born in December 2014. They started "Dwelling Ministries" in 2015. Dwelling's mission statement is: "Welcoming the presence of God to permeate every part of society."

In August of 2004, immediately before returning to Asbury College for my junior year, God intervened in my life in a radical way and rescued me from a life of destruction. Throughout that school year I began to know God through prayer, reading the Bible, and fellowship with other believers. No one had a greater impact on my life than the seventeen-year-old freshman I met that fall, Charis Miller. She was God's word of grace to me in living flesh, and she continues to be to this day, as my wife, Charis Spann. There seemed to be a growing interest on campus for the things of God during the 2004-2005 school year, but matters really began to escalate in the fall of 2005.

At a retreat in the summer of 2005, a spiritual mentor of mine said he sensed that God was about to take me into "deeper waters." This proved true as the fall semester began. The end of that summer had been a time of seeking God more intently than ever, and this search carried over into the school year. Immediately I connected with others on campus who had been experiencing a deeper work of God's Spirit. A friend of mine approached me about starting a Thursday evening prayer meeting. We did this in the World Gospel Mission Center (WGM) near campus, and it became a powerful part of God's activity at Asbury for the next two years. Other prayer gatherings started organically on campus. There was a growing hunger for God among a portion of students, and we could feel the spiritual momentum increasing.

Dr. Steve DeNeff came to speak at the Asbury annual fall revival services that September. The Holy Spirit seemed to work through his messages to pull on students' hearts and turn them to God. My cousin and my youngest brother, both Asbury basketball players, were ones whose lives were forever changed that week. This week of services just added to the spiritual fervor on campus. More students were seeking God, and with more passion.

Another important part of the prayer meetings and spiritual focus at Asbury was the influence of the International House of Prayer (IHOP) in Kansas City. This ministry, which has been facilitating worship and prayer twenty-four hours a day, seven days a week since 1999, was a source of spiritual supply for many of the "God-seekers" on campus. IHOP's music, teaching, and emphasis on worship and prayer were instrumental in fueling the flames of renewal.

There was a focus in prayer meetings to seek Jesus Himself and a cry for God to pour out His Spirit on our campus. Small groups met and prayed for this. Students talked about these things over meals in the cafeteria. Some would talk and pray in the dorm rooms all night until 7:00 in the morning in their pursuit of God. This was the spiritual climate of Asbury College in the Fall of 2005. Of course not everyone had the spiritual focus or hunger, but there was a definite contingent among the students who did.

During the winter break I traveled with four other Asbury students to the annual One Thing Conference in Kansas City. This gathering, part of the IHOP ministry, took place during the final four days of December 2005. Each of us experienced God powerfully in Kansas City. I personally was impacted in a way that still affects my life. We returned with fresh grace to impart and it was as if we carried live coals from God's altar to fuel the fire on campus.

My intensity of seeking God exploded upon my return and I could not get enough of His presence. I continued to join in with others as we sought Him corporately and then would spend hours a day seeking Him privately. The drive I felt from God's Spirit soon led me to the decision, not without challenge or cost, to step off the Asbury basketball team. Even as team captain and a teammate to both my brothers, I couldn't deny the overwhelming pull of the Holy Spirit. The day I announced this to my coach and team, the Lord led me into an extended water fast. This was the end of January and the spiritual momentum on campus was continuing to grow.

By this point two of my close friends had started what we called AHOP, or the Asbury House of Prayer. We would meet during the weekdays to pray and worship at the original Asbury building, the white "house" in the middle of campus. There were organized time slots to ensure at least someone was praying throughout most of the days and into the nights. Our prayer meetings continued on Thursday evenings at the WGM Student Center, but other than this, the AHOP building became the nucleus of prayer for the campus.

The last weekend of January and the first few days of February saw more heavenly help come to Asbury from God's servants in other places. First, a group from Georgia called First Love Ministries visited and brought spiritual breakthrough for the campus. Their praise, prayers, and declarations of God's word added a needed element to our work. Then, later that week a group of leaders from IHOP traveled from Kansas City because they had heard about the stirrings at Asbury. They encouraged us in our pursuit and they attended our weekly prayer meeting that Thursday.

The atmosphere of our prayer meeting at the WGM Center on Thursday night was charged with electricity. There were strong cries from students that seemed to have an extra empowerment from the Spirit. Some had tears, some groaned loudly; all at the meeting were sincere and focused. One of the highlights that night was gathering in prayer around my cousin, Brett Johnson, who was scheduled to speak in the student chapel service the following Monday. As we prayed for him and his upcoming testimony, God's power and presence were very tangible. It seemed that things were coming to a spiritual tipping point. The following week proved that this was the case.

I awoke Monday morning, February 6, and went to enjoy a nice breakfast in the cafeteria. My fast had just ended and this was going to be a big day. We had student chapel that morning starting at 10:00 a.m., but I had to be there a bit early because I was going to have a part of the service. After breakfast I returned to my dorm room before heading to Hughes Auditorium. I found myself praying at my desk with a fresh sense of ease and intensity. It really felt as if the Spirit was praying through me with groanings too deep for words. Before I knew it, it was time for me to leave for Hughes.

The students involved in leading the service that day gathered for prayer in the corner of the auditorium, as was customary for these services. Then we took our places on the stage in preparation for the service to begin. As the worship team led in songs of worship, I looked out at the faces of the students. I felt moved almost to tears when seeing a friend of mine lifting his hands in worship with an expression of absolute sincerity. The time of singing came to an end, and it was my responsibility to introduce the student speaker. I approached the podium with the desire in my heart to say just one word, the name of Jesus. I stood behind the microphone and looked out at the sea of faces. There seemed to be an extra grace of attentiveness to God's Spirit in the room. I spoke slowly and clearly, "Jesus, Jesus, Jesus. He is the reason we are here." I didn't say much beyond this other than introducing one of the student speakers that day, my cousin Brett.

When Brett came to the podium he gave testimony about what God had been doing in his life. After speaking, he played an audio track from the preaching of Corey Russell, a leader at IHOP in Kansas City. It was an intense moment of the service. Another student, a young lady, also testified of God's work in her life. During this time I was having a personal spiritual conflict as I could feel the resistance from the enemy's camp to what God wanted to do. I remember the spiritual opposition was strong. But God proved Himself stronger.

Toward the end of the service, the worship team was leading in song and the students seemed truly engaged. Some were already kneeling at the altar. I went to the podium to close in prayer. As I prayed I saw more students coming down the aisles to the altar. Others were in their seats with heads bowed. After praying, I saw one of my basketball teammates who had resisted God in days past, kneeling at the altar. I did not hesitate to go down and pray for him. He wept and was visibly touched. As I looked around, I saw that the auditorium was still full and I heard the music continuing. Immediately I went to pray for two other teammates who were in their seats. They had similar reactions to the first. After this, I scampered around Hughes like a kid at Christmas, excited to be free to minister to all that wanted God's touch. People were ministering to one another in various places around the room, and there was a large student gathering in front of the stage with their hands raised in worship.

The sweet presence of God's Spirit permeated Hughes Auditorium that Monday, and His presence continued to abide throughout the week. One of the aspects of this atmosphere I remember most was the freedom I felt. I remember dancing in the aisle as I worshiped that week and feeling so free to go pray for others as I was led. Although I had only known the Lord for a little over a year, I felt "at home" in this environment, and very much in my element. Some testified at the microphone onstage to what God was doing in their hearts. Some students confessed backsliding and sinful actions. Others exhorted the campus with words of corporate encouragement. Soon, people from outside campus came to see what was happening. Many people stayed in Hughes for hours at a time, and for days students were in the room around the clock.

The precious atmosphere of Hughes did not continue beyond that week in the same measure. God's tangible presence seemed to gradually lift from the room by the beginning of the following week. However, He still continued to move on campus in more subtle ways, and for some, the week of February six had lasting results. Although there had been a presence of prayer and worship carried by some for years before that school year, there was something unique that transpired during those days. It was as if God breathed into the campus a fresh breath during the 2005-2006 school year that would pave the way for a new sustained culture of prayer and worship at Asbury. This organic presence has continued to the current time at Asbury University.

Paul Rader - 2006

INTRODUCTION: Since Dr. Rader was President of Asbury University in 2006—at this time of writing the year of the most recent spontaneous revival—it is only fitting that we allow him final words.

In 2006, the final year of my presidency at Asbury, there was another spontaneous moving of God's Spirit on the campus. Here again students had been carrying a burden for revival, unbeknown to most of the campus community. They had been meeting for extended times of prayer and urgent intercession. I had preached in chapel the week before the breakthrough came. I could sense we were on the cusp of awakening, but was not free to open the altar.

The following week students led the chapel. Travis Spann, who had been a leader in the prayer movement for revival, opened the chapel simply by calling on the name of the Lord Jesus: "Jesus! Jesus! Jesus!" There was an immediate and electric sense that something was about to happen. A student followed with a sincere and moving witness. And then the fire fell.

The altar filled with weeping seekers. The aisles began to fill. Some were flat on their faces as they cried out to God. Many took off their shoes with a sense that they were kneeling on holy ground. The Spirit of the Lord filled the room. Students were reluctant to leave when the hour ended. While some left out of necessity, there were many who decided that what was happening there and then had the priority. The auditorium was full throughout the day and into the night. Into the early hours of the next day students continued to seek the Lord. Students, one after another, shared their hearts, sometimes confessing, sometimes exhorting, sometimes leading in earnest prayer. Musicians appeared to carry the worship. One had a sense that the Spirit was in control. Some faculty and staff were on hand throughout this time. We listened closely to what students were sharing as they responded to the Spirit's leading. There seemed little need to intervene or redirect what was occurring. It began with students and it continued to be a student-centered movement. One was reluctant to touch what was so evidently the Spirit's work. As in earlier awakenings on campus, as word reached other schools and churches in the community, many joined us in the evening hours. This continued unabated through most of the rest of the week, coming to some conclusion at the final chapel of the week. It was an awakening, a divine visitation of God, a refreshing and renewing movement of the Spirit. God had come once again to set Asbury Halls Aflame.

CONCLUSION: Dr. Rader wrote the following comments for the spring 2006 issue of Ambassador Magazine, sent to alumni, parents and friends of the University.

> *It is appropriate to feature our outstanding science department in this issue when we are reveling in the moving of God's Spirit in revival blessing across the campus. For what happens in Hughes Auditorium at the great altar of prayer is not divorced from what transpires in the classroom in the demanding and disciplined business of learning. "Academic Excellence and Spiritual Vitality" are not two distant or even concomitant concerns. They are all a piece of the whole as the pursuits of the classroom and laboratory are suffused with an awareness of the Lordship of Christ over all created reality. E. Stanley Jones, Class of 1907, used to speak of a surgeon friend who averred that he found the Kingdom of God at the end of his scalpel.... In every academic discipline we can celebrate the reality that Jesus Christ is Lord of all.[1]*

[1]Paul A. Rader, "Vital Faith and Disciplined Learning," *Ambassador*, Spring 2006, p.3.

Anna D. Gulick - 1970, 2015

INTRODUCTION: Though it largely relates to 1970, this piece appears at the end because it addresses the frequent question of why revivals seem to wane over time.

Professor Anna Gulick was fifty-one years of age and teaching French at Asbury College in 1970. Her parents were "devout" atheists whose dictum was, "Science has proved there is no God and it is not moral to believe what you know is not true." But forbidding Anna to speak about God did not prevent various relatives from speaking to God about Anna. She became a believer and then a missionary to Japan.

There she encountered colleagues who were a part of the 1949 Hebrides revival, a work that came in response to the praying of two elderly sisters who prayed every night before their peat fire for a move of God in their "godless parish." She recollected late in her life, "For 10 years after that I prayed to see revival with my own eyes. It was no accident that in 1970 God moved on campus at Asbury College. God had brought me there to witness that event."[1] Here are portions of a letter sent to family and friends in August 1970.[2]

Without any question, the biggest event since my last letter is the Asbury revival, which broke out in chapel on February 3. For me it did not begin with Tuesday chapel, but the Sunday before in my own church. Pastor Mount had preached on "touching the hem of His garment," and my own heart was so hungry for a fresh touch of His presence that I had to get home as fast as possible after the service so people would not see I had been crying. There I flung myself on my knees and cried out to God that I just couldn't wait any longer for the revival I had been praying about for fifteen years....

On Tuesday, instead of using his turn to address chapel, Dean Reynolds introduced an informal chapel of singing and voluntary student testimonies. Some of these testimonies were remarkable, both for the depth and for the number of "hard-core rebels" who told of the life-changing grace of God they had recently experienced....

I began to sense we were on the verge of something very big. As our President, Dr. Kinlaw, expressed it in retrospect, "These things aren't easy to explain. God simply walked in, and He has been here ever since."

Again and again the testimony was repeated that God's love had become tremendously real to an individual. Again and again different ones testified to having been given an overwhelming love for people they just "couldn't stand" before.

"School as usual" was totally out of the question. If classes had tried to meet, teachers could not have taught or students studied. We could not talk of anything but God and the work He was doing. Somehow word spread, by phone, by letter, by word of mouth. For the first several days it was next to impossible to get a long distance line out of Wilmore, and the electronic static was filled with references to "God," the "Holy Spirit," and "Revival." Wednesday revival broke out in the Asbury Seminary chapel. Thursday it leaped to the west coast where Azusa Pacific College had sent for one of our students to come and witness. Now the most recent report I have is that something like 1,500 witness teams have through June visited some 135 universities and states and have gone into hundreds of churches and public high schools across the nation. Also, Asburians have visited Africa, France, Japan, and several Latin American countries as well as in Canada, both by faculty and students. As I write, one professor is in Alaska, and another in Honduras....

I hope I may be pardoned a few more lines on the revival, as I know some of you are very much wanting my personal reactions. The most overwhelming memory of the great first week is of the Shekinah glory of God resting on everything, but particularly "presenced" to us in Hughes Auditorium. Most precious to me were the still hours of the night watches.

NOTE: *Writing in 2012, she indicates that during the first day of the 1970 revival God instructed her to go home at 6 p.m., eat supper, and go to bed... after setting her alarm for midnight. At first she inwardly protested. "I was afraid I would miss out on something, but God was insistent, so I obeyed." She assumed the "night shift," staying through "the wee hours" until a female teacher or matron appeared in the morning to help with counseling and prayer. Her 1970 letter continues.*

Few mere spectators remain between 3:00 a.m. and February dawn. We who were there, enclosed in the presence of God, were seekers after His face, those who had newly found grace, those who had come to give praise, those who were there to pray with or for others, those who came simply to worship. And the Shekinah was heavy upon us all. One night a young man kneeling beside me and still to all outward appearance the hippie he had been up to twenty-four hours before, breathed out: "O God, I am so grateful You let us come into Your life!"

The first few days I saw quite a bit of emotional and, in my opinion, unscriptural activity, but none of us quite dared touch it. However, in three days God Himself had straightened it out; for the most part everything that was just aberration dropped away. There I learned one of the most important lessons of the revival to me: God is still sovereign. The fires He lights He can trim.

By the end of the first week another very strong impression had come to me. Have you ever seen a time-lapse photographed movie in which many hours are compressed to just minutes, and you can see a flower seed germinate, sprout, wiggle upward, bud and bloom in a matter of seconds? That is how it was watching those who were babes in Christ on Tuesday suddenly grown up by Friday to a maturity some of us have never reached, and perhaps never will. Those born or significantly touched by the revival quickly acquired a stamp of God, a winsome sweetness in witnessing, a genuine burden for the lost and suffering, and a boldness in prayer unlike anything I have ever seen except in lives stamped in other great moves of God.

The change in climate on campus is most remarkable. I doubt if you could find a campus anywhere in the world with more genuine love and mutual trust between faculty and students. There is a freedom in speaking about spiritual things and about personal needs.

CONCLUSION: Years later, Anna wondered why the revival cooled. "Lives that were touched then are still bearing fruit all over the world. But I am also witness to the fact that the awesome presence of God we knew then is no longer there, and I have had to grapple with why."[4] The grappling is apparently over, for Anna is no longer with us.

The Rev. Anna. D. Gulick (M.Div., 1983), age 96, was born on Wednesday, September 11, 1918, and passed away peacefully in Wilmore, Kentucky, on Friday, August 21, 2015. She was a single missionary in Japan after World War II. She has mentored and provided support for many ATS students and alumni. We give thanks for her life and her ministry[5]

Now that she has gone to be with the Lord, Anna may have altogether forgotten her questions. The divine presence is purported to affect people in such ways (Revelation 21:3-4). In the meantime it is good to remember that God's work occurs on the mountains, in the valleys, and in the "ordinary" times of life. John Wesley's final deathbed words were, "The best of all is, God is with us."

Where It All Begins
Over the years I have come to a very strong conviction about revival:
It begins with God alone.
It is always preceded by prayer.
But I do not believe God gives revival because men pray.
I believe that when God is going to bring revival,
God sets his children to praying
to prepare the way...
If there is a burden for revival,
we have a right to believe that that burden is from God.[6]

Anna D. Gulick

[1]Anna D. Gulick, "The Need for a Prayer-Driven Church," Anglican Church in North America, http://www.anglicanchurch.net/?/main/page/254 (accessed 3/3/16).

[2]Anna D. Gulick, Letter, in AU Archives, Box 3.

[3]Anna D. Gulick, *Captured: An atheist's journey with God* (Lexington, KY: Emeth Press, 2012), p. 147. *[NOTE: "atheist's journey," small case, is part of original title]*

[4]Anna D. Gulick, "The Need for a Prayer-Driven Church."

[5]Obituary of Anna Gulick, Asbury Theological Seminary, Alumni e-link, http://elink. asburyseminary.edu/alumni-obituaries-september-2015/ (accessed 4/2/16).

[6]Anna D. Gulick, *Captured,* p. 140-141.

ADDENDA

ADDENDUM #1 Asbury Revivals at a Glance

YEAR	START DATE/TIME	START PLACE	PRESIDENT	# DAYS CLASSES SUSPENDED
1905 A	Feb.	Chapel—MECS[1]	J. W. Hughes	Extended
1905 B	Oct.	Chapel—MECS	B. F. Haynes	Extended
1907	Feb. 17 / 10 p.m.	Student Room	B. F. Haynes	Seven
1908	Feb. 18	Wesley Basement	Nelson Wray	Two (services lasted 2 weeks)
1916	Mar. 3 / Evening	Wesley Basement	H. C. Morrison	Unknown
1921	Feb.	Chapel	H. C. Morrison	Unknown
1932/1957[2]	Spillover / Unknown	Africa	Does Not Apply	Does not apply
1938	Jan. 27 / Thur. Noon	Dining Hall	H. C. Morrison	Unknown
1942	Oct.	Dining Hall	Z. T. Johnson	One
1950	Feb. 23 / Thurs. 9 a.m.	Hughes Auditorium	Z. T. Johnson	Three (Th.-Sat.), 119 cont. hours.
1958	Mar. 1 / Sat. 8 a.m.	Hughes	Z. T. Johnson	One (Sat.), 63 cont. hours.
1970	Feb. 3 / Tues. 10 a.m.	Hughes	D. Kinlaw	Five (Tu.-Sat.), 144 cont. hours.
1992	April 3 / 10 a.m.	Hughes	E. G. Blue	One
1995	April 3 / 7 p.m.	Hughes	D. J. Gyertson	One
2006	Feb. / Mon. Chapel	Hughes	P. A. Rader	One (5 nights)

[1]MECS - Methodist Episcopal Church, South, Chapel, Wilmore, KY

[2]Story largely taken from an account in the then Belgian Congo, stemming from records of Asbury graduate, Dr. Alexander Reid. *[NOTE: Dr. Reid explicitly states that inspiration for the 1931 prayer with fasting movement was inspired by his experience of revivals at Asbury.]*

YEAR	SPONTANEITY[3]	NAME ONE KEY FIGURE	EXTERNAL IMPACT
1905 A		E. A. Ferguson	
1905 B		Benjamin Haynes	
1907	High	Eli Stanley Jones	Mega Revival[4]
1908		W. P. Gillis	
1916		Boys' Conference Members	
1928		John Paul	
1932/1957[2]	High	Alexander Reid	Mega Revivals
1938		Joseph Owen	
1942		Dwight Ferguson	
1950	High	Robert Barefoot	Mega Revival
1958		Leon Fisher	
1970	High	Jeannine Brabon	Mega Revival
1992		Roy Lauter	
1995		Wheaton Team	
2006	High	Travis Spann	

[3]Spontaneity indicates a revival that totally surprised the majority of the participants and did not occur in conjunction with previously scheduled activities.

[4]"Mega" Revival is a somewhat subjective designation, based on factors like duration, external impact, suddenness, reports in the secular or religious press, representative of a wider nationwide movement of spontaneous campus revival, and so forth.

ADDENDUM #2
Extraordinary Dispensations of Providence:
Twentieth Century Spontaneous Revivals at Asbury College

Presented to the Southeastern Section of the Evangelical Theological Society, March, 1979, by Harold E. Raser, Division of Philosophy and Religion, Asbury College

On May 30, 1735 the young Connecticut minister Jonathan Edwards penned a letter to a fellow minister in Boston describing an unusual stirring of religious consciousness that was becoming evident among the inhabitants of the Connecticut River Valley to whom he ministered. He declared that this work:

> Seems to be upon every account an extraordinary dispensation of Providence. 'Tis extraordinary upon the account of the universality of it in affecting all sorts, high and low, rich and poor, wise and unwise, old and young, vicious and moral; and also on the account of the quickness of the work of the Spirit on them, for many seem to have been suddenly taken from a loose way of living, and to be so changed as to become truly holy, spiritual... persons... 'Tis extraordinary as to the extent of it, God's Spirit being so remarkably poured out on so many towns at once and its making such a swift progress from place to place.[1]

The "extraordinary dispensation of Providence" that Edwards recounted with such wonder in this "Narrative of Surprising Conversions" was shortly to reach floodtide and would leave in its aftermath thousands of new Christians, scores of reawakened ones, new churches, increased philanthropic and humanitarian activity, missionary work among the American Indians, and a common concern for higher education that would spawn such universities as Princeton, Dartmouth, Brown, and Rutgers.[2] Indeed it was a "Great Awakening," as historians have dubbed this eighteenth-century religious and social revival.

It was not to be America's only such awakening, however, for other unusual quickenings of spiritual concern had occurred throughout the nation's history and have taken their place alongside this first and been labeled successively a "Second Great Awakening," a "Third" and even a "Fourth Great Awakening."[3] The first of these "Great Awakenings," of which Edwards found himself a part, broke out suddenly and spontaneously, taking placid New England communities by surprise. Likewise, the "Second Great Awakening," though it became focused and organized around several great personalities, grew out of scattered spontaneous "showers of refreshing," one of which drenched Yale University in 1801 and resulted in the conversion of one-third of the students, many of them headed to influential preaching and teaching posts.[4]

By the end of this Second Awakening, one of its chief exponents, Charles Grandison Finney, was declaring that in the future Christians ought not to passively wait for the moving of God's Spirit in unusual ways, but ought rather to plan and prepare and bring about revivals by using certain "constituted means" ordained by God for this very purpose. So far from being miraculous, "A revival," declared Finney, "is a purely philosophical result of the right use of the constituted means—as much so as any effect produced by the application of means."[5] Increasingly reflecting Finney's frame of mind, America's subsequent times of revival have tended to become less spontaneous, more highly orchestrated from the outset, centering around specific means and techniques, notably the rural campmeeting and its various urban offshoots. God has no doubt been pleased to use these means, as a recounting of the history of "revivalism" in America would show, though on occasion He has circumvented them to still manifest His power in "surprising" and unexpected ways. This can be illustrated by reference to a rather remarkable series of religious awakenings at a small Kentucky Christian liberal arts school, Asbury College.

Integral to the founding of Asbury College was a philosophy of religious revival which held that periodic times of spiritual refreshing for Christians and clear opportunities for conversion of the unsaved are essential to the well-being of the Christian Church, and by extension to the health of the Christian college. In harmony with Finney's beliefs about the use of means and measures to bring about such revival times, Asbury College has from its earliest days scheduled special religious services each academic year. In this sense one could say that Asbury experiences "revival" every year; certain "constituted means"—to use Finney's phrase—are used to bring about deepened or new spiritual commitment among students and faculty on a regular basis. If this were all, Asbury would be scarcely distinguishable from a host of evangelical Christian colleges which employ similar means on a regular basis. Asbury claims our attention, however, because on several notable occasions during its eighty-nine year history the earlier American pattern of spontaneous, unplanned spiritual renewal—more akin to Edwards's "extraordinary dispensations of Providence" than to Finney's "right use of the constituted means"—has asserted itself unmistakably.*

EDITOR'S NOTE: Dr Raser's assessment holds weight, but perhaps there is some simplification in representing Finney himself. For in spite of a more "orchestrated" approach, he was deeply committed to "travailing" prayer (Psalm 126: 5), and marvelously used by God.[6]

[1]Jonathan Edwards, "The Great Awakening," *Works of Jonathan Edwards, Volume IV*, edited by C.C. Goen (New Haven, CT: Yale University Press, 1972), p. 107.

[2]H. Shelton Smith, Robert T. Handy, and Lefferts A. Loetscher, *American Christianity, Volume I* (New York: Charles Scribner's Sons, 1960), p. 314.

[3]William G. McLoughlin, Jr., *Modern Revivalism: Charles G. Finney to Billy Graham* (New York: Ronald Press, 1959), p. 8. *[NOTE: He suggests limits for these as First Great Awakening, 1725-50; Second, 1795-1835; Third, 1875-1915, Fourth, 1945ff.]*

[4]Sydney E. Ahlstrom, *A Religious History of the American People* (New Haven, CT: Yale University Press, 1972), p. 416.

[5]Charles G. Finney, *Lectures on Revivals of Religion*, edited by William G. McLoughlin, Jr. (Cambridge, MA: Belknap Press of Harvard University, 1960) p. 13.

[6]David Thomas, *To Sow for a Great Awakening: A Call to Travailing Prayer.* (Franklin TN: Seedbed Publishing, 2016), pp. 6, 15, 27.

To access the entire document - Asbury University Archives, Asbury Revivals, Box 1, File #1.

ADDENDUM #3

Our Biblical and Wesleyan Heritage Through Fasting and Prayer[1]
By Alexander James Reid

For more than half a century I have believed that God graciously rewards all of His people who are willing to take the time and pay the price to fast and pray until victory comes. I have glanced through my own diaries and noted outstanding times when the miracle working of Christ moved in mighty power in the hearts of men and women in Africa and America. In every case, those times have been preceded by days or years of fasting and prayer. I have written at length about the most fruitful event in my Congo ministry. After two years of fasting and weeping and praying, the Holy Spirit moved upon thousands of hearts in the Congo. Its influences are still going on.

When called upon in September 1972 to speak at the Lake Junaluska meeting of the International Prayer Fellowship, with some 300 delegates from all over America, including among them many of the leaders of the Key 73 movement, I felt led to tell them about the Congo Experience. The Holy Spirit moved upon that assembly.

When we returned to our home in Wilmore, Kentucky, I felt definitely led of the Lord to start Fast Prayer Meetings every Friday from twelve till one o'clock in Hughes Auditorium. From week to week we have met with a group composed of some Wilmore residents, students, and professors from both Asbury College and Asbury Theological Seminary to share in that hour of blessing. I have been led to search the Scriptures and the journals of our Methodist leaders to learn more about this biblical and historical practice and to share with others what I have learned from this study.

Hundreds of requests have come from people across the nation for this pamphlet on *Fasting and Prayer*, and many have pledged God to begin fasting prayer groups in their churches and communities. One church board promised to have commitment cards printed which would enlist individuals and groups to enter into a covenant with God for periods of fasting and prayer.

Individuals and groups have written the President of the United States to follow the lead of President Lincoln 100 years ago, who called for a day of National Fasting and Prayer. Others reminded him that at the approach of our 200th anniversary as a nation we should follow the lead of Wesley's England, which for five consecutive years from 1777-1781 had National Fasts when "all shops were closed, all places of public worship were filled, and no food was served in the King's palace until after five o'clock."

We should continue to pray, meet the conditions and expect the fulfillment of the promise of 2 Chronicles 7:14: *"If my people who are called by my name shall humble themselves, and pray, and seek my face and turn from their wicked ways: then I will hear from Heaven and will forgive their sins, and will heal their land."*

The Bible has much to say about fasting and prayer. The word "fast" is used 20 times; "fasting" 17 times; "fasted" 13 times. Let us look into some of these Scriptures.

Neh. 1:4," *When I heard these words, I sat down and wept and mourned certain days, and fasted before the God of heaven."*

Isaiah 58:6, *"Is not this the fast that I have chosen? To loose the bands of wickedness, undo the heavy burdens, and to let the oppressed go free, and that ye break every yoke?"*

Ezra 8:21, *"Then I proclaimed a fast at the Ahava that we might afflict ourselves before our God, to seek of Him a right way for us, and for our little ones, and for our substance."*

Psalms 109:4, *"My knees are weak through fasting."*

Joel 1:14, *"Sanctify ye a fast, call a solemn assembly, gather the elders and all the inhabitants of the land into the house of the Lord your God, and cry unto the Lord."*

Joel 2:12, *"Therefore thus saith the Lord, turn ye even to me, with all your heart, and with fasting and with weeping and with mourning, and rend our heart, and not just your garments, and turn unto the Lord your God, for He is gracious and merciful, and slow to anger and of great kindness and repenteth Him of the evil."*

CHRIST CONCURS AND EXPECTS NOTHING LESS THAN THIS OLD TESTAMENT STANDARD FOR HIS CHURCH OF OUR DAY

Christ fasted forty days and forty nights.
Matt. 4:2, *"And when he had fasted forty days and forty nights, he was afterward an hungered."*
Matt. 6:16, *"When ye fast...."* Christ implies in this chapter that all of His people will give alms, will pray, and will fast.
Mark 9:29, *"And he said unto them, this kind can come forth by nothing but by prayer and fasting."*

THE APOSTLE PAUL WRITES OF HIS TIMES OF FASTING

1 Cor. 7:5, *"...give yourselves to fasting and prayer...."*
2 Cor. 6:5, *"In stripes, in imprisonments, in tumults, in labours, in watchings, in fastings."*
2 Cor. 11:27, *"In weariness, in painfulness, in watchings often, in hunger and thirst, in fastings often, in cold and nakedness."*

WESLEY'S COMMENTS ON FASTING

The following quotations are taken from my copy of *Wesley's Journal* published in the year 1837 as arranged by John Emory:

Friday, Feb. 17, 1744. "We observed a day of solemn fasting and prayer. In the afternoon, many being met together, I exhorted them to make to themselves friends of the mammon of unrighteousness, to deal their bread to the hungry, to clothe the naked, and not to hide themselves from their own flesh." (pg. 313)

Wednesday, Dec. 18, 1745. "Being the day of the PUBLIC FAST, we met at four in the morning. I preached on Joel 2:12. At nine our services at West Street began. At five I preached at the foundry again on, 'The Lord sitteth above the water clouds.' Abundance of people there." (pg. 361)

Friday, Feb. 16, 1750. "We had a solemn fast day meeting, as before at five, seven, ten and one." (pg. 475)

Friday Feb. 6, 1756. "The fast day was a glorious day; such as London has scarce seen since the Restoration. Every church in the city was more than filled; and a solemn seriousness on every face. Surely God heareth prayer." (p. 595)

Friday, Dec. 28, 1757. "We observed a solemn fast; and from this time the work of God revived in Bristol." (p. 646)

Friday, Feb. 17, 1758. "The PUBLIC FAST. I preached at West Street in the morning at Spitalfields in the afternoon, and Bull-and-Mouth in the evening; everywhere to a crowded house. Indeed, every place of worship throughout the city was extremely crowded all day long. Surely all the prayers which have been offered this day will not fall to the ground." (p. 649)

Thursday, Apr. 13, 1758. "I explained at large the nature and manner of entering into covenant with God and desired all who were purposed to do so, to set FRIDAY apart for solemn fasting and prayer. Many did so, and met both at five in the morning, at noon, and in the evening." (p. 652) *[NOTE: The date is wrong in Reid's original listings. Thursday, Apr. 13, 1758 is correct. See* The Works of John Wesley, *3rd Edition, Thomas Jackson, ed. Vol. 2, 1978, p. 439.]*

Friday, Feb. 12, 1762. "The NATIONAL FAST was observed all over London with great solemnity. Surely God is well pleased with this acknowledgement that He governs the world; and even the outward humiliation of a nation may be rewarded with outward blessing." (p. 315)

Friday, May 24, 1771. "I spoke severally to the members of the Society at Limerick. We observed this a day of fasting and prayer, and were much comforted together." (p. 351)

Friday, Aug. 9, 1776. "Our conference began and ended on Friday which we observed with fasting and prayer, as well for our nation as for America." (p. 459)

Thursday, Aug. 16, 1776. "I went out to Launceston. Here I found the plain reason why the work of the Lord had gained no ground this circuit all the year. The preachers had given up the Methodist testimony. Either they did not speak of perfection at all (the peculiar doctrine committed to our trust) or they spoke of it only in general terms, without urging believers to go on unto perfection, and expect it every moment. And wherever this is not earnestly done, the work of God does not prosper." (Wesley's Works, Sermon CXVI p. 459).

Friday, Jan. 13, 1777. "Was the NATIONAL FAST. It was observed not only throughout the city, but throughout the nation, with utmost solemnity." (p. 466)

Friday, Feb. 27, 1778. "Was the day appointed for the NATIONAL FAST: and it was observed with solemnity. All the shops were shut up; all was quiet in the streets; all the places of public worship were filled; no food was served in the King's house until five o'clock in the evening." (p. 482)

Wednesday, Mar. 10, 1779. "It was a day of NATIONAL FAST. So solemn a one I never saw before. From one end of the city to another, there was scarce anyone seen in the streets. All places of public worship were crowded in an uncommon degree; and an unusual awe sat on most faces. I preached on the words of God to Abraham, "I will not destroy the city for his sake." (p. 502)

Friday, Feb. 4, 1780. "Being the NATIONAL FAST, I preached first at the new chapel and then at St. Peters, Cornhill. What a difference in the congregation! Yet out of these stones God can raise up children unto Abraham." (p. 523)

Wednesday Feb. 21, 1781. "Being the NATIONAL FAST, I preached in the new chapel in the morning, and at the West-Street in the afternoon. At this as well as at the two last public fasts, all places of worship were crowded; all shops were shut up; all was quiet in the streets, and seriousness seemed to spread through the city." (p. 538)

Friday, Feb. 25, 1789. "The day in which I ordered our brethren in Great Britain and Ireland to observe with fasting and prayer."

Although this was the last reference made on fasting and prayer in John Wesley's Journal before his death, I want to quote a statement from one of his sermons on fasting and prayer. "While we were at Oxford, the rule of every Methodist was (unless in case of sickness) to fast every Wednesday and Friday in the year, in imitation of the primitive church *[NOTE: In this context "primitive" means early]* for which we had the highest respect. 'Who does not know,' says Epiphanius, an ancient writer, 'that the fast of the fourth and sixth days of the week (Wednesday and Friday) are observed by the Christians throughout the world?'" (Wesley's Works, Sermon CXVI)

Concerning the time of such fasts, Wesley indicated that the early Christians abstained from all food and drink during the fast days until after three in the afternoon.

Since we should be systematic in our prayer life, Bible study, and in giving of offerings and tithe, so should we be systematic in our times and days of fasting. No matter where we are or with whom, we should observe the fast and not eat. Certainly all of us have much to learn about this sacred privilege and obligation of fasting. The more we study the Bible, and the more we read in the biographies and journals of outstanding Christian leaders of the early Church and the impact which they left on the times in which they lived, the more we realize how much we ourselves are missing in not practicing this God-ordained means of grace. It enables God in some mysterious and remarkable ways to do what otherwise He does not do.

I have reviewed the life of our first American bishop *[NOTE: "American" as in the first bishop born in America]*, William McKendree. From his diary I quote a few passages:

Wednesday, Sept. 22, 1790. "In the morning I spent an hour on my knees in fervent prayer, reading God's Word, and praising my adorable Saviour. It was a time of heavenly joy to my soul. From ten o'clock to half past one o'clock, I spent in a lonely swamp in wrestling, agonizing prayer. But surely God and his Holy ones were all around me. Heaven burst into my bosom, and Glory filled my soul."

Friday, Sept. 24, 1790. "Having to ride some fifteen miles and preach, I had some temptation to breakfast, but resisted them: and though I suffered on account of abstinence, yet the cross vanished, and I suffered less than usual on fast days. Praise and power, honor and glory to God—the meeting lasted four hours, when one of the mourners sprang up, and praising God for snatching him as a brand from the burning. O, how like heaven is the place where God revives His work."

The author of *Life and Times of Bishop Wm. McKendree* wrote, "The practice of fasting at regular intervals, it is feared, is, like some other very excellent usages, among the old Methodists, becoming less strictly observed of late than formerly. The habit among preachers especially, was to fast every Friday, some added Tuesday—and those who were too feeble to fast throughout the entire day, abstained until evening. The quarterly fasts were kept by all the members. Bishop McKendree was punctual and rigid in all these observances."

If Dr. Paine who wrote on the life of Bishop McKendree, felt that there had been a departure among the Methodists of his day from some of the early observances, what would he say today if he were among us?

Let us try to envision what could happen on the American continent if Christ's people who are called by Christ's name, Christian, would humble themselves, seek God's way and FAST AND PRAY until our whole continent with its national leaders, would feel impelled of God to call NATIONAL DAYS of fasting and prayer, as happened in Wesley's England in that day. Suppose on such days of a NATIONAL FAST all our houses of worship were filled to their capacity with people praying and all the stores were closed and our streets empty. We would be able indeed to call our continent to Christ and to win our continent for Christ. Is such an effort worthwhile? Let us test out God's wonderful promises, and prove Him there with until He would pour out His heavenly blessing on our needy land.

Recognizing that all of us are busy with many calls upon our time we cannot fill, from this biblical and historical evidence, perhaps we should rearrange our *priorities* and give God more time to help us. Surely in such times as these, with the series of crises we as a nation are facing, with religious journals writing "Are we nearing the last Holocaust?", should we not seriously consider systematic times for FASTING AND PRAYER as our first priority of our lives?

All for Christ and a world-wide revival,
Alexander J. Reid, Wilmore, KY – 1972

[1]Asbury University Archives, Alexander T. Reid, Manuscript Collection, Box 63, Folder 7.

ADDENDUM #4
A Final Word of Grace

Along the Via Salutis (the way of salvation) why would revival be necessary even at historic Christian colleges like Asbury? Despite a faithful remnant, the lights may grow dim, running the gamut from hedonism to legalism, often more pervasively and subtly than realized. Think of Adam and Eve slinking from the garden in remorse. In one generation, Cain defiantly denies all wrongdoing under divine interrogation. Think of a thriving Pauline church at Ephesus, losing its first love by the time of the Revelation. In his own lifetime Wesley saw telltale signs of compromise with Mammon among Methodists.

And the story persists in individuals, families, churches, institutions, and societies once friendly to the gospel of Christ. Sin in the human heart is cunning and overpowering. Despite their best intentions, God's people often wander and fail. More tragic still, they do so without knowing it until—like Samson—the Philistines are upon them.

But there is good news. Divine love is deeper than sin and failure. God knows all that is wrong with us and loves us in spite of it, perhaps even more because of it. Sin may run deep, but the blood of the cross goes deeper. Because of grace people may dare to come to the light; revival is possible. Prodigals are welcomed home (Luke 15); revival is beautiful. Thanks be to God!

Selected Bibliography

Books

Baldwin, Ethel May and David V. Benson. *Henrietta Mears and How She Did It*. Glendale, CA: G/L Publications, Regal Books, 1966.

Beougher, Timothy and Lyle Dorsett, eds. *Accounts of a Campus Revival: Wheaton College 1995*. Wheaton, IL: Harold Shaw Publishers, 1995.

Coleman, Robert E. and David J. Gyertson. *One Divine Moment: The Account of the Asbury Revival of 1970,* 25th Anniversary Edition. David J. Gyertson, ed. Wilmore, KY: First Fruits Press, 2013.

Coleman, Robert E. *The Master Plan of Evangelism*. Grand Rapids, MI: Fleming H. Revell, 1963.

Collins, Kenneth J. and Jason E. Vickers, eds. *The Sermons of John Wesley: A Collection for the Christian Journey*. Nashville, TN: Abingdon Press, 2013.

Duewel, Wesley. *Revival Fire*. Grand Rapids, MI: Zondervan Publishing House, 1995.

Edwards, Jonathan. *"The Great Awakeing," Works of Jonathan Edwards, Volume IV.* C. C. Goen, ed. New Haven, CT: Yale University Press, 1972.

Elliott, Stephen D. *By Signs and Wonders: How the Holy Spirit Grows the Church*. Franklin, TN: Seedbed Press, 2016.

Finney, Charles G. *Lectures on Revivals of Religion*, William G. McLoughlin, ed. Cambridge, MA: Belknap Press of Harvard University, 1960.

Foster, Robert D. *The Navigator, Dawson Trotman (forward by Billy Graham)*. Colorado Springs, CO: NavPress, 1983.

Graham, Billy. *Just As I Am: The Autobiography of Billy Graham*. New York: HarperCollins, 1997.

Gulick, Anna D. *Captured: An atheist's journey [sic] with God*. Lexington, KY: Emeth Press, 2012.

Hamilton, Adam. *Revival: Faith as Wesley Lived It*. Nashville, TN: Abingdon Press, 2014.

Heitzenrater, Richard P. *Wesley and the People Called Methodists*. Nashville, TN: Abingdon Press, 2013.

Hughes, John Wesley. *The Autobiography of John Wesley Hughes, D.D., Founder of Asbury and Kingswood Colleges, with Biographical Contributions by Rev. Andrew Johnson, D.D., Ph.D. and Appreciations by Others*. Louisville, KY: Pentecostal Publishing Company, 1923. Reprint ATS, Wilmore, KY:First Fruits Press, 2013.

Jackson, Thomas, ed. *The Works of John Wesley*, 3rd Edition (reprinted from the 1872 Edition). Grand Rapids, MI: Baker Book House, 1978.

James, Henry C. and Paul Rader. *Halls Aflame: An Account of the Spontaneous Revivals at Asbury College in 1950 and 1958*. Wilmore, KY: Asbury Seminary Press, 1966.

Jones, E. Stanley. *A Song of Ascents: A Spiritual Autobiography*. Abingdon Press: Nashville, TN, 1968.

Lovelace, Richard S. *Dynamics of Spiritual Life: An Evangelical Theology of Renewal*. Downers Grove, IL: Intervarsity Press, 1979.

Maddox, Randy L. and Jason E. Vickers, eds. *The Cambridge Companion to John Wesley*. New York: Cambridge University Press, 2010.

McConnell, Lela, with Edith Vandewarker. *The Mountain Shall be Thine*. Jackson, KY: Kentucky Mountain Holiness Association, 1989.

McKinley, Edward. *A Purpose Rare: 125 Year of Asbury University*, Ed Kulaga, editor. Ann Arbor, MI: Edwards Brothers Malloy, 2015.

McPheeters, Chilton C. *Pardon Me, Sir... Your Halo's Showing: The Story of J. C. McPheeters*. Wilmore, KY: Francis Asbury Press, 1984.

Morris, Danny and Sam Teague. *The John Wesley Greet Experiment: The Story of the John Wesley Great Experiment*. Franklin, TN: Providence House Publishers, 2001.

Nicholi, Armand M., Jr. *The Question of God: C. S. Lewis and Sigmund Freud Debate God, Love, Sex, and the Meaning of Life*. New York, NY: Free Press, Simon and Schuster, Inc., 2002.

Norwood, Frederick. *The Story of American Methodism: The History of United Methodists and Their Relations*. Nashville, TN: Abingdon Press, 1974.

Oden, Thomas C. *John Wesley's Teachings, Four Volumes*. Grand Rapids, MI: Zondervan, 2014.

Orr, J. Edwin. *Tongues Aflame: The Impact of 20th Century Revivals*. Chicago, IL: Moody, 1973.

Raymond, Jonathan S. *Higher Higher Education*. Spring Valley, CA: Aldersgate Press in Collaboration with Lamp Post, Inc., 2015.

Richardson, Michael. *Amazing Faith: The Authorized Biography of Bill Bright*. Colorado Springs, CO: Waterbrook Press, 2000.

Tennent, Timothy. *Invitation to World Missions: A Trinitarian Missiology for the Twenty-first Century*. Grand Rapids, MI: Kregel, Inc., 2010.

Thacker, Joseph. *Asbury College: Vision and Miracle*. Nappanee, IN: Evangel Press, 1990.

Thomas, David. *To Sow for a Great Awakening: A Call to Travailing Prayer*. Franklin TN: Seedbed Publishing, 2016.

Wesche, Percival A. *Henry Clay Morrison, "Crusader Saint."* Anniversary Edition. Wilmore, KY: Asbury Theological Seminary, 1963. [Digital: http://place.asburyseminary.edu/firstfruitsheritagematerial/24/].

Periodicals and Digital

"Francis Asbury: Pioneer of Methodism, America's Most Explosive Church Movement." *Christian History*, Issue 114, 2015.

Asbury University Archives.
http://www.asbury.edu/offices/library/archives.

Acknowledgements

This anthology was a team effort (though any errors or omissions belong solely to the editor). Living contributors took time to discuss and write about their experiences. The deceased cared enough while living to reflect on events and record them. We are the beneficiaries.

Alongside biographical contributors stand numerous supporters. First, thanks to past Asbury College Presidents Dennis Kinlaw, Paul Rader, and David Gyertson for conversational time and support. Second, I acquired deep appreciation for patient copy editors, among whom are Norm Styers, Skip Elliot, Jonathan Kanary, and especially Beth Gardner (who was also my World Literature professor many moons ago). General encouragement and advice came from Robert Coleman, Jonathan Raymond, Phillip Collier, Jiles Kirkland, Bob Wiley, Penny James, and Jeff James. I savor memories of friendship and coffee at Solomon's Porch.

Since college days, I had tinkered with the idea of residing again in Wilmore. That wish came true for two summer months through cooperation of departmental staff in Asbury Administration and Alumni Relations. I received gracious assistance from Jeanette Davis, Carolyn Ridley, Lisa Harper, Liz Stephan, and many others. Network relationships also coalesced at Asbury Seminary: librarian Janice Huber, professors Robert Stamps, Stephen Seamands, Steven O'Malley, and Kenneth Collins, who allowed me to sit in on the Wesleyan Studies Summer Seminar.

In 2014 I remarked to Archival Director Suzanne Gehring, "Why has no one developed a more comprehensive review of Asbury revivals?" She smiled, "Maybe you should." She and her staff provided invaluable research support.

Special thanks to Seedbed Press editor Andrew Miller, who introduced me to Kyle Schroeder, a designer and media producer. Finally—next to my children and irreplaceably supportive wife, Lynne—I am indebted to Skip Elliot for sharing advice, meals, his home, a love for history and Asbury, and his passion for God's glory.

Author Bio – Robert J. Kanary

Robert "Bob" Kanary is a longtime United Methodist pastor in the Oklahoma Conference of the United Methodist Church and an endorsed chaplain with the Division of Higher Education.

Dr. Kanary holds degrees from Asbury College (1974, BA History), Oral Roberts University (1980, Master of Divinity), and Fuller Theological Seminary (1988, Doctor of Ministry). His dissertation title was *The Sunday Service: Focal Point and Catalyst for a Process of Spiritual Formation, Lay Ministry, and Kingdom Growth.* In 2000 he proposed and conducted a pilot study for the UPPER ROOM, using the daily devotional guide as a basis for small group discipleship. The proposal was modified and is now included in each issue.

Besides pastoral ministry, he is involved with the Navigators, a parachurch ministry which—along with other efforts—developed the follow-up ministries for the Billy Graham Evangelistic Association beginning in 1950. He is laboring on a related book with the proposed title, *John Wesley Meets the Navigators: Biblical Principles of Discipleship for Every Generation.*

Bob is interested in childhood literacy, having published *How Tortoise Helped Jack Rabbit Win Too*, a story book designed to motivate adults to read aloud with children. He has served as an officer in the Oklahoma City chapter of the C.S. Lewis and Inklings Society.

He enjoys music, the Master Gardener program, basketball, and walking outdoors in the early morning. Bob and Lynne have two adult children, Jonathan, an Anglican minister (ACNA) working on a cross-disciplinary Ph.D. in Religion and Literature at Baylor University, and Sara, who is a professional counselor (LPC).

Bob entertains hopes that *Spontaneous Revivals: Asbury College 1905-2006* may be used by God to nourish fresh stirrings of God's Spirit in a thirsty world.

Made in the USA
Monee, IL
27 January 2020